BRUTAL
BOSSES

and Their Prey

ALSO BY HARVEY HORNSTEIN

Social Intervention: A Behavioral Science Analysis

The Social Technology of Organizational Development

Applying Social Psychology

Cruelty and Kindness

Managing Human Forces in Organizations

*Managerial Courage: Revitalizing Your Organization
Without Sacrificing Your Job*

*A Knight in Shining Armor: Understanding Men's
Romantic Illusions*

BRUTAL BOSSES

and Their Prey

How to Identify and Overcome Abuse in the Workplace

HARVEY A. HORNSTEIN, Ph.D.

RIVERHEAD BOOKS

New York

RIVERHEAD BOOKS
Published by The Berkley Publishing Group
200 Madison Avenue
New York, New York 10016

Riverhead hardcover edition: March 1996
First Riverhead trade paperback edition: October 1997
Riverhead trade paperback ISBN: 1-57322-586-X

The Putnam Berkley World Wide Web site address is http://www.berkley.com

The Library of Congress has catalogued the Riverhead hardcover edition as follows:

Hornstein, Harvey A.
    Brutal bosses and their prey/ by Harvey A. Hornstein.
        p.   cm.
    Includes bibliographical references.
    ISBN 1-57322-020-5
    1. Employees—Abuse of. 2. Executives—Professional ethics.
3. Cruelty. 4. Hostility (Psychology) I. Title.
HF5549.5.E43H67   1996   95-39652 CIP
331.25—dc20

Printed in the United States of America
10   9   8   7   6   5   4   3   2   1

CONTENTS

INTRODUCTION

Bosses who mistreat subordinates are subjecting them to special torment. In buses, trains, planes, stores, streets, and stadiums, victims of incivility are free to reject such abuse and either demand proper conduct or exit the situation. At work, the combination of bosses' power and subordinates' dependency limits access to these options, forcing the prey of brutal bosses to suffer their humiliation in silence.

My eyeglasses were resting on my boss's desk, near where I was seated. I'm nearsighted and usually remove them when I'm reading. His face was beet red. I could actually see the veins on his neck from where I sat, three or four feet away. It was really ugly.

Suddenly he picked up his pad, saying something like "You couldn't see anything even if you had them on," and he hurled it. The pad smashed against my eye-

glasses, ricocheting them hard into the wall. They were destroyed.

I was in shock and said something dumb like "What have you done?"

"I've done nothing. Now get out of here and get that information back to me in presentable condition by four this afternoon."

It's all well and good to talk about being brave, but when instead of another job offer you have a pocketful of college loans due and a kid on the way, as I did, all that was left for me was to pick up my shattered glasses and my shattered ego and do what I was told. I was angry, but I was also trapped. I'm not embarrassed: I'll tell you, I was so frustrated that my eyes filled with tears, and they are right now, again, just because I'm telling you about this.

Information gathered from nearly a thousand working men and women over an eight-year period reveals the awful consequences of this silent suffering for both individual victims and the organizations in which they work. My sources were American and international, wealthy and broke, with membership in most major industries, including manufacturing, communications, insurance, entertainment, law, agriculture, computers, education, publishing, advertising, government, petrochemicals, and finance. Representatives from every organizational level took part, their ages ranging from twenty to seventy.

The batteries of standard diagnostic questionnaires that most participants completed gave me and my colleagues objective indices of both the unexpectedly high frequency with which brutal boss behavior occurs and its adverse effects on subordinates. Their contributions were made anonymously, but they know who they are. Data that these sources provided show that abusive disrespect by bosses is commonplace, apparently on the increase, and certainly detrimental to its victims' mental and physical health.

The objective evidence supplied by these working people was supplemented by the stories that hundreds of other employees provided in writing and through interviews. Some were former clients and students whom I knew as a consequence of my work during the past two and a half decades as an organizational consultant, management educator, and professor in the social-organizational psychology graduate program at Columbia University, where we use behavioral science methods to understand and affect the consequences of group dynamics in work settings. Others were strangers corralled by former students and clients of mine who urged them to tell me their stories. And the rest were people I interviewed in luncheonettes, waiting rooms of all kinds, shopping malls, airports, supermarkets, and taxi cabs, whenever and wherever I encountered someone who had a personal and important tale to tell.

Spontaneously and in response to a series of questions, these men and women painted stirring and revealing portraits of what preceded their bosses' misconduct and of the aftermath for them, their bosses, and their organizations. They described the humiliation of public denunciations by bosses who sometimes seethed with quiet rage and other times erupted with screamed obscenities, vicious ridicule, name-calling, and even physical assault. I heard of bosses—lots of them—who spit, threw things, and smashed objects, some ordinary, some precious. Subordinates told me about how, facing threats that were extreme, frightening, and bizarre, they were commanded to provide demeaning and non-work-related personal services for bosses. And others described how their bosses engaged in rudeness, lying, favoritism, and sleazy dealings at their expense. As much as possible, while remaining a vigilant guardian of respondents' anonymity (and thus I've changed names and identities), I present their narratives without alteration.

Their stories touch every page of this book. They demonstrate that the nineties are an extraordinary breeding ground for brutal bosses, and help to establish the differences between "tough" bosses and abusive ones, between cruelty due to organizational pressure and for personal pleasure. It is these honest reports from the field that point to the link between bosses' abusiveness and the effects on subordinates' well-being and productivity; that prove the perversity of organizations that punish victims of abuse while protecting—and promoting—abusers; and that show the dangers of such modern workplace innovations as electronic surveillance. Ultimately, the contributions of nearly a thousand strangers illuminate the bold and vital path to a workplace based on fairness and free of abuse.

Some fundamental level of civility is a requirement of human conduct that neither ends nor diminishes when the workday begins. Bosses who are mean to subordinates are not merely violating some effete rule of social etiquette, they are actually causing measurable injury to both their individual victims and to the institutions in which they and their victims work. Bosses' cruelty adversely affects employees' initiative, commitment, motivation, anxiety, depression, self-esteem, and productivity, and may also be implicated in the occurrence of headaches, heart disease, gastrointestinal disorders, sleep disturbances, dermatological problems, sexual dysfunction, and even murder.

And it is on the rise.

"Organization spirit is being crushed," says Billie Alban, an organizational consultant who has been honored more than once by both the American Society of Training and Development and the Organization Development Network. Recently, when Billie and I directed a conference together, she asked sixty senior human resource professionals to draw, as best they could, a representation of the spirit in their organizations. Spontaneously, without a spoken word, the room filled with individual depictions of the Grim Reaper; drawings of dark, huddled figures descending into ominous places; sketches of dangerous, engulfing seas; graveyards and sunsets.

This is a turbulent time for organizations. The changing characters of competition, downsizing, workforce demographics, customer demands, and popular images of leadership serve to either ignite abuse in otherwise reasonable bosses or unleash it from predisposed organizational bullies. The statistics are staggering. An estimated 90 percent of the workforce suffers boss abuse at some time in their careers. On any given workday, as many as one out of five subordinates report to bosses from whom they expect harmful mistreatment.

In an effort to remedy brutal boss behavior, some advisors suggest that organizations teach subordinates methods intended to blunt their suffering. Others recommend the introduction of training programs and performance evaluations that encourage bosses to restrain their toxic behavior. Both of these approaches are likely to fail because they focus on changing individuals, either the innocent victims or their abusers, without making any attempt to change the organizational environment that shapes their tragic encounters. Any meaningful effort to discourage the abuse of subordinates requires reformation of work arrangements according to a new social compact, one that gives all employees a genuine voice in designing their operating environments and that deconstructs traditional work hierarchies and their stifling obsession with power.

Evidence exists that organizations are experimenting with these progressive work arrangements. There is talk of using new, empowering managerial tools—flattened hierarchies, self-managed teams, participative decision-making, circular personnel structures, quality circles, "seamless" organizations, process re-engineering, "whole system interventions," "360-degree feedback." Unfortunately, lots of bosses talk in such fancy terms about workers' autonomy but behave autocratically. There is firm evidence that progressive work systems actually change the daily lives of very few employees—as few as 10 percent, by one estimate—and that the politics and perversions of organizational life form a natural barrier to their broad application. Wider use of empowering work innovations merits everyone's support; yet something more is required. Brutal boss behavior must be outlawed.

Companies and businesses bear obligations to the communities that host them as well as to their investors. They are not free to act contrary to their communities' economic and physical well-being, and they should not be free to act contrary to the psychological and vocational well-being of the people in those communities who work for them.

In the United States, organizations already have a legal obligation to prevent the misconduct of those they invest with power over others. Bosses are not permitted to behave in ways that produce a hostile, intimidating, or abusive work environment for an employee because of the employee's race, age, religion, gender, disability, or national origin. This organizational duty should be extended. It must ultimately apply to all employees, not only to some.

No one deserves to be treated cruelly, and no one is immune to the degradation of body and spirit caused by on-the-job abuse. When injuries result from worksite exposure to chemical substances, the offending institutions are compelled to introduce remedies. When the injuries originate from toxic human behavior, no less should occur. Communities everywhere have an obligation to ensure that organizations are held accountable for the hazardous consequences of misbehavior by brutal bosses, and the organizations themselves must fulfill their duty to diligently monitor, limit, and rectify any occurrence of abuse.

On the contrary, most of the employees who contributed to *Brutal Bosses and Their Prey* said that their organizations, perversely, tend to protect abusers and condemn the abused. It was often painful for these informants, battle-worn and disillusioned, to recount ugly episodes of boss abuse. Some cried, others shook their heads in disgust, and more than a few swung their fists at empty air, as if their oppressive superiors were still standing there. I thank all of them for their efforts, and hope that what this book discloses about brutality by bosses—its causes, consequences, and cures—can help to restore their emotional health and dignity.

In collecting data, I was greatly helped by Lauren W. Cohen, Wendy L. Heckelman, John L. Michela, Maggie Sachse-Skidd, Janet L. Spencer, and Ann M. Van Eron. They were wonderful colleagues, and I pray that I was a good boss, for they deserved no less. For a good portion of the eight years of research, these co-workers helped me also to design and validate the Brutal Boss Questionnaire, the diagnostic tool that appears as the book's appendix.

Thanks also to my agent, Gerard McCauley. For a decade, I have had the comfort of being cared for by his able and professional hands, which this time guided me to Putnam's wonderful Riverhead Books. There I worked with my terrific editor, Nicky Weinstock. Wow, what an experience.

I am not convinced that my two youngest daughters, Alison and Erica, would shout the same gleeful "Wow!" to characterize the experience of being around me when I work. They dutifully tiptoed through the house and listened with diplomatically disguised impatience as I described one or another of each day's surprises or insights. A "thank you, Alison and Erica" would be superfluous: They already know how grateful I am that they are my daughters.

Jessica, my third daughter, is a married woman with a home of her own. She escaped the burdens that this book imposed on her sisters. But she also knows how truly grateful I am to have her as my daughter.

Madeline E. Heilman, to whom I have been married for more than two decades, is a co-professional who never let her personal achievements and busy work life stop her from carefully reading every page of *Brutal Bosses,* as she has done with each one of my books, or from providing me afterward with hours of eye-opening commentary. This book is dedicated to my wife.

CHAPTER ONE

DISRESPECT:

Poisoning the Workplace

As he passed by the glass wall of my office, his silhouette was clearly visible on the thin, filigreed curtains. The shadow had almost no detail, but my boss's gait was unmistakable. As the handle started to turn, even before the door opened, I sensed what was going to happen. It had been a while since I was "in the barrel," and it was about to be my turn again.

Almost anything could set him off. That's what made it so awful—you never could predict just when it was going to happen. There might be a piece of work with a minor error, or no error at all, but he just wouldn't like it the way it was. Or he might chuck you in the barrel because of a disorderly desk—not necessarily yours—or a telephone call that you couldn't answer because of a meeting *in some other part of the facility, or because you were in the loo.*

Don't imagine that I'm speaking to you about some wild-haired screamer. This fellow was a typical mid-forties, blue-suit type, balding, with a slight belly. Really, a Mr. Everybody: attaché case, kempt, with kids; an orderly, work-gets-done-on-time type.

"Billy," he said, standing in the doorway so that everyone in the central area could see and hear us clearly. "Billy, this is just not adequate, really not at all. We want to do better than this." He was speaking very slowly and quietly, as if I were a three-year-old. As he spoke he crumpled the papers that he held. My work. One by one he crumpled the papers, holding them out as if they were something dirty and dropping them just inside my office as everyone watched.

Then he said loudly, "Garbage in, garbage out." I started to speak, but he cut me off. "You gave me garbage. Now you clean it up."

I did. Through the doorway I could see people looking away because they were embarrassed for me. They didn't want to see what was in front of them: A thirty-six-year-old man in a three-piece suit stooping before his boss to pick up crumpled pieces of paper.

THE FACTS

Fact: Billy's experience is not unusual. Statistical evidence shows that in today's organizations, abusive disrespect of subordinates by their bosses is commonplace —among workers like Billy, who makes $47,000 a year in a government agency, and among high-level executives who make five times his salary. More than 90 percent of the people I interviewed judged that more than 90 percent of working women and men experience abuse at some point during their careers. On any given day, as many as 20 percent of employees report to abusive bosses.

Fact: Billy's boss is likely to continue behaving in the same way in the foreseeable future, unchecked and probably protected by the organization as long as he "meets the bottom line."

Fact: With continued exposure to his boss's abusive behavior, Billy and anyone else thrown "in the barrel" will very likely suffer adverse physical and mental symptoms accompanied by lowered work productivity.

Billy's suffering is a typical consequence of experiencing a boss's abuse, as documented in empirical evidence gathered from many hundreds of other working men and women like him. Such suffering screams to us that respectful boss behavior is a necessity, not a nicety, of work life.

In organizations, we *earn* income, promotions, and perks, but we are *entitled* to respect. Hostile personal attacks, threats, ridicule, and humiliation trash an irrevocable right that we all possess: the right to be treated according to accepted standards of human relations and fairness. In social settings outside of work, these kinds of interpersonal abuse threaten to injure pride and deface self-images. But when the abuse is inflicted by a boss on a subordinate, the threat is multiplied because accompanying power dynamics tend to discourage any redress. The organization commonly protects abusive bosses while punishing employees who are their victims.

Disrespectful behavior is a social toxin. It paralyzes its victims, draining energy, initiative, and desire while undermining their physical and psychological well-being. There might be a perverse comfort, if it were true, in attributing this widespread tragedy solely to the behavior of bosses whose sick personalities made them brutal. But it's not true. Such bosses certainly exist, possessed by core characters that are malignant and cruel, and we will examine them and their actions. But the spread of abuse's poison cannot be blamed entirely on bad personalities. Bosses are just you and me. Subordinates are most often bosses as well, and may be guilty—despite their justifications—of the same abusive disrespect toward their subordinates that they lament in their bosses. Conditions, as well as character, are what prod bosses of all types toward brutality. Organizational power hierarchies, competitive work climates, and the bunker mentality of contemporary corporate life all provide a hospitable environment for the toxin of disrespect, and even induce it, from bosses who would otherwise be just.

Many who have recognized the horrible effects of this toxin offer advice to the rest of us on how to deal with it. They tell us either to avoid exposure—*change your work schedules so as to limit contact with your boss,* and *take special care to work around a boss's pet peeves*—or they advise us on how to live with the pain—*focus on your strengths,* they urge, or simply, *meditate.* This advice is nonsense. Even if there were effective ways of insulating oneself from an unrelenting barrage of humiliating and degrading boss assaults (which evidence and common sense suggest is not generally possible), the counsel is focused in the wrong direction. Abusive boss behavior itself is the problem, not the work patterns and reactions of the people it afflicts, and it must be stopped. There should be no victims.

If the abundance of this toxin in our work lives is a natural product of how organizations are currently functioning, then one answer is obvious: Let us demand change in the way organizations work. The toxin of bosses' cruel disrespect is causing harm to employees just as other toxic products cause harm. The fact that this particular toxin is human rather than chemical is of little consequence to those who suffer its effects, and should not absolve organizations of their responsibility to eliminate it from workplaces.

Proscribing abusive behavior in workplaces and holding organizations accountable for its occurrence is hardly without precedent. Title VII of the Civil Rights Act signed into law in 1964 bans all discrimination based on race, religion, or national origin in workplaces. That rule was extended to discrimination based on age in 1967, gender in 1972, and pregnancy in 1978. In 1986, the United States Supreme Court ruled that *sexual harassment* is a form of discrimination. The Equal Employment Opportunity Commission, created by the 1964 Civil Rights Act, defined behavior in workplaces as harassment if it produces a *hostile* or *intimidating* work environment, hinders individuals' work, or adversely affects employment opportunity. In fact, regardless of the target person's ethnicity, age, gender, or physical condition, abusive disrespect of subordinates by bosses does exactly what the law prohibits: It creates a hostile, intimidating

work environment that hinders subordinates' performance and adversely affects their future employment opportunity.

Admittedly, harassment of others due to their membership in these designated social groups is prohibited because it would perpetuate a preexisting pattern of civil
rights abuse. For this reason alone, the forms of behavior
proscribed under Title VII deserve the special legislative
and judicial attention they have received. Nonetheless,
from the perspective of human experience and well-being, abuse is abuse. Many of the most insidious consequences of the abuse suffered by Billy and millions of
others are no different from those suffered by victims of
mistreatment declared illegal more than thirty years ago.

In response to my inquiries about mistreatment on the
job, a significant percentage of working men and women,
sadly, shared experiences of abuse that were explicitly
religious, gender-based, and racial. Gwen, for example,
told me of her first "real" job, at twenty-five, when she
worked for a human resources group in a pharmaceutical
firm. Shortly after joining the firm she was assigned to a
newly organized work group, an exciting opportunity for
her—which she mentioned to her new boss, Henry, a
man of about forty. Henry expressed his pleasure in return and spoke with Gwen about working together.

*What Henry did not explain to me during that orienta-
tion was that he would regularly, in public and private,
make open guesses about the quality of my sexual experiences the night before. He would say, "Looking good! I
bet it was okay last night," or "What's the matter? A little
down today—not enough action?" Then he'd laugh and*

*wink. It was rude and embarrassing. No one said any-
thing . . . and neither did I. He was the boss, after all. I
went to any extreme to avoid him, so it was affecting my
work. Finally, I spoke to a woman, another supervisor in
our division at his level. She said, "He does it all the
time. Forget it. He likes you. You're lucky he isn't trying
to get you to spend the night with him."*

*Can you believe it? She was protecting him and warn-
ing me! It couldn't have been clearer. I was the underling
who was supposed to accept these insults. They were
sexist, but they could have been about anything and no
one would have cared. It was disgusting. How could I
forget it? I was sick with humiliation but wanted to do
well in the company. It was a dreadful time for me.*

Hostile environments exist when racist jokes are whis-
pered and sexual innuendo becomes the stuff of public
and demeaning conversation. But hostile environments
also exist when any employee becomes the target of disrespectful behavior by more organizationally powerful
others. Abused employees suffer, and their plight should
not be neglected simply because their mistreatment is
not the result of belonging to a specifically protected social category.

As members of the social community at large, every
one of us is entitled to fair treatment from our fellows,
regardless of differences that may exist among us, including job title, educational background, wealth, gender,
race, attractiveness, competence, intelligence, waist size,
or office size. Oppressive boss behavior violates this
right, damages its individual victims, and ultimately
cheats companies of productivity.

TOUGH IS NOT ABUSIVE

Some of the people who spoke to me put on their "boss hats" and told me of times when they had actually treated subordinates with disrespect. The tone of these remarks varied from matter-of-fact to obvious embarrassment. No one, however, admitted to being politically incorrect: There were no self-reports of bosses who had harassed employees because of their religion, gender, race, national origin, or physical disability (despite the fact that about 15 percent of the abuse reported to me by workers fell into these categories). Some who had served as bosses defended their behavior toward subordinates by claiming that getting a job done often requires a boss to be *tough*. This brings us to the distinction that must be made between *tough* and *abusive* bosses. Abusive bosses who claim that "toughness" was required are engaging in a self-serving cover-up.

Paul B. Kazarian is the ex-CEO of Sunbeam-Oster. His treatment of subordinates apparently had something to do with the addition of the "ex-" to his title. Mr. Kazarian admitted to being "unbelievably demanding" and a "perfectionist," according to an article in *The New York Times*.[1] He is quoted as stating that these are the qualities in him that his subordinates disliked, a conclusion that is evidently incorrect. Subordinates instead found him intimidating, volatile, and intolerant, abusive to the point of throwing things when they displeased him. Sunbeam comptroller Henry Rauzi, for example, was the target of an orange juice container pitched by Mr. Kazarian, who was upset over an error that Mr. Rauzi may have made. Such an act presumes status, authority, and a privilege vis-à-vis the other that has nothing to do with simply being demanding and perfectionist. This assault is certainly not something that people would expect to get away with in a social group where they did not have a power advantage. Behaving this way toward others is not simply being tough, it's out-and-out abusive.

After assuming control of New York City's *Daily News* in 1993, Mortimer Zuckerman also apparently thought that he was simply being tough when he met with his new subordinates and advised them, "If you stay here and work for me and you're productive, you can be as hard on me as you want and I'll respect you," but faced with a worker who is not productive, he vowed "he would punish the employee by kicking his behind, using a more common expression."[2] Mr. Zuckerman's promises and threats communicate that his subordinates receive basic respect only according to their production, not because they are adult members of the same human community that houses Mr. Zuckerman. Now, lack of productivity in organizations certainly deserves an administrative response; work settings are not welfare systems for employees. But there were other options open to Mr. Zuckerman besides threatening to kick employees' behinds, just as there were for Mr. Kazarian when he allegedly threw the orange juice container. Dismissal, demotion, probation, and a mandate of remedial training could have been posited as consequences of deficient effort. All of these are reasonable sanctions for employee misbehavior, and all are appropriate in the workplace.

But threatening personal harm, even—perhaps especially —as a symbolic expression of intent, crosses the boundary of boss-subordinate relations by presuming a right to personally and flagrantly demean someone.

Mr. Zuckerman, Mr. Kazarian, and all other bosses should be commended when they set high, attainable standards for their subordinates. At issue are not the standards set but the breakdown of civility and the assault on human dignity that can occur in the course of enforcing those standards. Tough bosses with high goals may cause their subordinates to feel insecure and uncertain of their ability to achieve the required levels of performance; but, as you will see, there is clear evidence that the emotional and work consequences of that experience are very different from those that result from being bludgeoned, belittled, and betrayed by bosses.

A man told me the story of a female employee who came to him for help when he was working in the personnel department of his organization. The woman, a foreign national, explained to him that her boss was treating her in "uncivil" ways. Criticisms, she said, were shouted at her in public. She was called names and on several occasions had paper thrown at her. Her testimony about these events and others equally insulting was later supported by two people, an outside witness to the boss's behavior and the organization's investigator into the woman's complaint. This boss had a history of grievances about him; in fact, around the time that this woman complained, five people left the unit because of him. In time, the organization reassigned the woman— but, in the words of the man reporting the case, "not before her physical condition deteriorated. She looked aged, wrinkled, tired, and she said, 'My pride is destroyed.' " The boss continued in his job unscathed by the events.

Workers' rendition of the distinction between tough bosses and abusive ones is not unlike students' perception of two different kinds of teachers. Do you remember thinking, "Old So-and-so is tough . . . but *fair*"? Folks often work hard for those kinds of teachers. Life with them isn't easy because so much is demanded, but students feel neither terrorized nor denigrated by their strictness. The "Old So-and-so's" of this world are different from other teachers who, with and without high standards, belittle students, reward them unjustly, and punish them arbitrarily. These are the ones whose classes you may have anticipated with waves of fear and stomach pains. Such symptoms are no wonder, because these teachers exploded unpredictably, put students "in the barrel," and engaged in name-calling, until threat of humiliation hung constantly over the classroom like a guillotine's blade.

An assessment test of thirty-six questions that my associates and I administered to many hundreds of working people provides you with a clear method of distinguishing tough bosses from those who are abusive. The test is included as the book's appendix to help you, when considering your own boss, to draw a line between tough and abusive and determine whether it's been crossed. Taking the time now to complete the questionnaire at the back will enable you to identify objectively which type of superior is yours. The two kinds of bosses, like the two kinds of teachers, have very different effects on their subordinates. Adverse states of mental health and decreased job satisfaction are not associated with reporting to a demanding taskmaster, but are likely results of reporting to a boss who is a master of cruel disrespect.

Bosses are us, and we are never supposed to be discourteous, impolite, or uncivil. Conventional gestures of greeting and farewell are expected to be extended and reciprocated. Lying is forbidden. Threats are frowned upon. Yelling, cursing, name-calling, and physical attack all meet with varying degrees of disapproval in relationships among people who possess common respect for one another.

Relationships between adults begin with the assumption of some level of mutual and unconditional respect. This common right does not end when the workday begins. Disrespectful boss behavior is, by definition, always inappropriate. It violates universal social prescriptions and prohibitions and breaks the rules of decency that form the heart of any community. My investigation has revealed that these transgressions by disrespectful bosses fall into eight categories. Hundreds of respondents confirm that employees expect bosses not to commit any of the Eight Daily Sins listed below, regardless of their or their subordinates' personal attributes—status, ability, wealth, education, or performance—and regardless of any organizational conditions or crisis. These are sins when they are visited by any boss at any time in any situation upon any subordinate, and their result is the stealing of dignity from the worker and the workplace.

THE EIGHT DAILY SINS

Deceit   Lying; giving false or misleading information through acts of omission or commission.

Constraint   Restricting subordinates' activities in domains outside of work, e.g., where they live, the people with whom they live, friendships, and civic activity.

Coercion   Threatening excessive or inappropriate harm for noncompliance with a boss's wishes.

Selfishness   Protecting themselves by blaming subordinates and making them the scapegoats for any problems that occur.

Inequity   Providing unequal benefit or punishment to subordinates due to favoritism or non-work-related criteria.

Cruelty   Harming subordinates in normally illegitimate ways, such as public humiliation, personal attack, or name-calling.

Disregard   Behaving in ways that violate ordinary standards of politeness and fairness, as well as displaying a flagrant lack of concern for subordinates' lives (e.g., "I don't give a damn about your family's problems").

Deification   Implying a master-servant status in which bosses can do or say whatever they please to subordinates because they feel themselves to be superior people.

Abuse is unacceptable at the workplace and beyond, but circumstances sometimes allow its victims outside the workplace to either reject or ignore it. For example, you can walk away from the incivility of strangers in supermarkets or on public transportation, even if you are walking away with temporarily gritted teeth and stomach knots. Or else, if the gritting and knotting prove unbearable, others' incivility can be rejected with a challenging comment, gesture, or action that rebukes the behavior and refutes the other's "right" to treat you without dignity.

The same responses are rarely feasible in work organizations. Power plays and employees' dependency can make them impossible. Many workers do not want to quit and cannot afford to be fired. Despite inspirational literature from progressive management theorists about companies whose managers walk about and stimulate creativity, commitment, and motivation in benevolently "flattened" hierarchies, the reality for millions of workers—including those in "progressive" companies—is that their bosses are disrespectful and abusive.

What makes Ralph's story so frightening is that so many of us have had similar experiences.

I was working as a tool and die maker and had a boss who was convinced that he knew more than anyone else about mechanics. Even though my work was praised by customers, he took evident delight in joking with other supervisors about my work and the work of others. After I built a machine for a department in the plant, he stood in the middle of the department and questioned the selection of the type of steel I had used. He did so disparagingly and in a cynical tone. When I tried to defend my work, he simply smirked and, in front of everyone, turned away.

In fact, turning away from me was the single most humiliating thing I can remember him doing. It was as if he was dismissing me from the human race. I was left standing there with my mouth open. I worked for this guy for a year after this. I was subjected to this disrespect from him for about sixteen months.

Many similar stories show how the resulting wound to self-pride goes unhealed because a boss's power stifles any meaningful redress. Many of these narratives also show how a boss's arbitrary abuse of power can be a threat to job security. But Ralph's insight about his sad experience provides wisdom about one of the most subtle consequences of a boss's disrespectful behavior: Ralph felt "dismissed from the human race." That is the nature of severe disrespect. In every social encounter, people express a verbal and nonverbal evaluation of others, either affirming or negating their worth, dignity, and equal human status. Bosses' disrespect communicates to its target, *You do not merit the common, minimum social courtesies that are due to other members of my community. You are less than us. I am more than you. You are dismissed.* The Talmud considers the public humiliation of someone an equivalent to death; Ralph, accordingly, felt dead.

Minority members know the experience of having their

worth and dignity discounted by bosses: "Hey you, *boy*" to a thirty-two-year-old African-American employee. "Whatsa matta, José, you no speaka the goo Henglish?" to a Hispanic man working as a CPA, whose name was in fact Hector. Women are also not strangers to experiences of disrespect that communicate, *You are not a full member of the community.* "Have the *girl* do it," said a department store boss within earshot of a saleswoman in her thirties. "Love the way you walk, you pretty little thing," from a boss to a woman who'd just landed their public relations firm's second-largest account. The consequences of these abusive encounters for minorities and women are tragic, and they are no less tragic when they are visited upon other members of society.

Ralph's suffering, typically, did not end with the humiliating encounter itself: "I was a bear to live with at home. My wife and I had been married for fourteen years at the time and we started having conflicts, engendered partially by my anger and feelings of dislocation." And it adversely affected his work behavior as he tried to heal his damaged pride in ways that were potentially destructive to him and the organization: "I would spend a half hour telling my wife how this dickhead had treated me during the day and talking about the strategies I was employing to work against him. I employed malicious compliance whenever possible and never missed an opportunity to disparage my boss with others in whatever forum presented itself. My main defense against the humiliation was to devote energy to combating him."

Disrespectful boss behavior should not be treated as if it were an inconsequential breach of etiquette. As Billy, Gwen, and Ralph confirm, it is much more. Work occupies a unique place in the lives of adults. Not only do they spend a great many of their waking hours at their jobs, the workplace also provides one of the few opportunities for adults to have contact with the same people day after day. When the most prominent person among them, one's boss, behaves with meanness and disrespect, it is an abuse of power that violates a universal social contract and poisons the workplace.

Bosses should not be free to do whatever they wish to subordinates. However, evidence and experience clearly indicate that they prey upon subordinates regularly and often with complete impunity because their power intimidates and silences their victims. When subordinates have daily doses of humiliation and cannot either escape or respond, the effect is toxic. What is at risk is nothing less than their physical and psychological well-being, in addition to their work productivity.

And abusive boss behavior has never been more abundant than it is in today's workplaces.

CHAPTER TWO

WORK IN THE NINETIES:

Bosses Under the Gun

Why all this whining? Why now, late in the modernized and sanitized twentieth century, are so many hundreds of workers driven forth to tell their stories of brutal bosses? After all, legislation, labor regulation, worker action, and social conscience have limited and, in many instances, reversed the spread of exploitive, unhealthy, and morally unconscionable work conditions. Length of workdays is limited, the use of child labor is restricted, and exposure to harmful chemical substances forbidden. Things on the whole have gotten much better. So why complain?

From the safe heights of historical perspective, adverse work conditions may seem less odious nowadays than they were during the faraway first years of the Industrial

Revolution. But to the subordinates in the trenches who are absorbing blows delivered by today's bosses, the pain is unmitigated by an academic overview of the history of labor. Fifty, one hundred, or two hundred years ago, work conditions in general may seem more inhumane when they are measured against today's workplaces, with our computers and labor unions and sophisticated talk of workers' rights. Yet today's employees are feeling pain because of mistreatment by today's bosses. Abstract comparison is not a remedy for daily suffering. Moreover, bosses now are operating in a context unique to the 1990s, whose pressures and effects create a psychological brutality on the job that was unknown in the past.

Aggression in response to threat is a common characteristic of many of this planet's organisms. Humans, including those who happen to be labeled "bosses," are a case in point. In fact, although a larger number of interviewees blamed their bosses' abusive behavior on proclivities in those supervisors' personalities, almost as many attributed the abuse to circumstances at work that were both stressful and threatening. Pressure on bosses— a specialty of this decade—can push them to mistreat subordinates with a frequency and vehemence that would be unlikely otherwise.

Take heed: This is not the beginning of an apology. Although bosses' stressful situations were identified as a major contributor to their abusive behavior by about 40 percent of respondents, these victims suffer no less than the subordinates of spontaneous abuse, and were not more forgiving—nor should they be. "It's inexcusable," one person wrote to me, "but sometimes people who are under pressure just lash out at someone who can't fight back, like the person who had a tough day at work and kicks the dog at night. Well, as Mr. K's subordinates, we're the dog. And when he's upset, which is often, we get kicked."

It's a widespread observation. When bosses feel pressed or threatened, they often demonstrate just how human they are by striking out (as many of the rest of us do) and taking aim at subordinates. The question, of course, is whether the nineties are special in terms of pressuring and threatening bosses. The answer is: *absolutely*. In fact, for many bosses, this decade is a white-knuckle nightmare because they and their organizations are under siege.

THE SIEGE MENTALITY

Luis, forty-three years old, is employed in the marketing department of an American automotive giant. He sighed as he told his story.

It was micromanagement with a vengeance, control-your-rest-room-break type stuff. He was brusque all the time, totally impolite, red-faced, and wide-eyed as he huffed and puffed his picayune, punishing criticism. I was suffering. My wife and kid were suffering. My back was to the wall. It felt as if I was being crushed and suffo-cated.

Driving to work one day, I said to myself, "Okay, that's it. I may have to move along, but he's got to be told. We're all being tortured to death, my co-workers as well as my family."

When I arrived I bumped into him, and we went up-

stairs together. I described how desperate the situation was, how he had changed since the downsizing and reorganization. He never denied any of it. You know what he said? "Fuck you! I got pressure on me that you wouldn't believe. I'm dying and you're crying. You count who's being kicked out into the street from this place: guys like me. And I've got to cover what I was doing and whatever gets dropped when they disappear. I've got no time for your bullshit. My ass is on the line and fuck you if you think that I'm going to worry about your ass."

Luis's story illustrates one cause of both the siege mentality that has gripped many bosses and the abusive disrespect of workers that is its result. As the world's economy worsens, cost-conscious organizational whittling carves away layers of supervision and management. For bosses, and everyone else who remains behind, a trimmed organization means a greater work burden. Survivors are expected to produce more with fewer resources. And as if all this weren't bad enough, another contemporary trend adds still more horror to bosses' nightmares: A modern management credo has redefined the requirements of being an effective boss to include the empowerment of subordinates. In short, today's bosses must do more with less, and do so *without* exercising the individual authority that once came with positions of greater responsibility and accountability.

Please recognize that I am not claiming bosses are actually fulfilling mandates of worker empowerment, only that many of them are under pressure—coming from the top and bottom of their organizations—to change their ways. For now, regardless of either the social gains that such changes represent or the financial benefits that some promise will accrue when the changes are accomplished, for bosses such a redefinition of their role adds further turbulence to the shake-up in 1990s organizations.

As Luis's story reveals, one major factor in the emergence of a siege mentality for his and other bosses is the downsizing of companies. The statistics that I provide below have been the subject of newspaper headlines for the last decade; therefore, I will present just a few numbers in order to illustrate how severely bosses have been threatened by recent cutbacks.

Employees in positions of authority have suffered disproportionately to their numbers during workforce reductions. Middle managers were feeling ill-treated by their employers even at the beginning of this decade. In 1990, only 43 percent of this group answered "yes" to the question of whether their companies treated them with respect; two years earlier, 51 percent had responded affirmatively to that same question.[1] It is an equally important and troubling fact that, at best, only half the managers surveyed ever felt respected by their employers. What has happened to these people during company efforts to downsize may offer some insight into their disillusionment.

In February 1993, a survey of 836 companies showed that although middle managers made up only 5 percent of the surveyed companies' workforces, they accounted for 22 percent of their layoffs.[2] This disproportion is similar to one that was reported two years earlier in a survey of 1,100 member companies of the American Management Association. In this earlier survey, middle managers represented between 5 and 8 percent of the companies' employees but 17 percent of the dismissals.[3]

More recently a focus group study[4] of the baby boom generation that now populates so many management positions revealed that work pressures resulting from downsizing have caused these workers to concentrate on their own job security and neglect subordinates' career development. Neglect of underlings, however, is not the only result of increasing work pressures: *Abuse* of them can provide bosses with the illusion of power and a sense of release in situations characterized by their powerlessness and by pressure, pressure, pressure.

Terry's story is just one example of a boss whose abuse of subordinates can be traced to the company's economically induced efforts at reorganization.

The restructuring left our boss with about half the staff, all the tasks that he had before, and tighter deadlines. He had more work, but it was a demotion—or soon to be one. The word was out, eventually in writing, that the restructuring would have negative consequences for future job grading and promotion opportunity. At first I felt sorry for Mr. Z. Everyone did, I think. He was sort of serious, conservative, with thin-lipped smiles, but in a kind of cool, distant way he was decent. I suppose he was insecure and shy. Then all that changed, both his decency and how sorry we all felt.

It was like Jekyll and Hyde. He was awful to everyone, literally throwing work at us. And he'd mutter about how stupid, sloppy, and incompetent we were. It got worse when the work really backed up. The added pressure put him on the edge and he really took it out on us, because he thought they'd taken away some of his clout and he needed to keep us toeing the mark. But I'll tell you, what he did had the opposite effect: He didn't respect us and we didn't give a damn about him.

The misbehavior of bosses gripped by the siege mentality is a matter of state, not trait. They do not necessarily thrive on harming those less powerful, as do the bosses featured in the next chapter, but rather feel that they must stamp down subordinates to stay on top of things and alive.

BOSSES VERSUS FACILITATORS

In the organizational world of the 1990s, titles such as *boss, supervisor, manager,* and the like have declining approval ratings, whereas *facilitator, coordinator, sponsor,* and *coach* are gaining popularity. The difference between the two groups of titles relates to authority. Boss-types issue commands that are meant to be obeyed. They see themselves as having decision-making authority because of their position in a fixed organizational structure that prescribes a chain of command. The facilitator-types, by contrast, aid *team* decision-making, expecting that participation will produce in subordinates motivation for commitment and thoroughness. In this way, inclusiveness and empowerment replace authority and obedience as the principle causes of productive subordinate behavior. For these "progressive" facilitator-types of the nineties, organizational structure is not a fixed mandate but a flexible tool, shifting in order to fit the jobs at hand. Priority is given to changing work needs, not to the maintenance of control over subordinate behavior through strictly enforced rules and roles.

Bosses are inclined to achieve performance standards by telling their direct reports what to do, how to do it, and by when it must be done. *Facilitators* aim to create a climate for quality performance by collaborating with subordinates to clarify job expectations, build a cooperative team, solicit input on ways to improve quality, provide performance feedback, and establish and communicate work standards. Ideally, the facilitators' preferred work setting possesses several distinctive characteristics in addition to its flexibility: a flattened hierarchy, pay systems that are skill-based and broadbanded, and, very possibly, self-managed teams.

New organizational models require new leadership skills. Facilitators, as opposed to bosses, are expected to be adept at *visioning*—expressing desirable and achievable future states—as well as at supporting, teaching, coaching, and developing teamwork. These are essentially replacements for bosses' tendencies to micromanage, control, and direct subordinates on a one-to-one, authoritarian basis.

Titles and jargon aside, today's bottom line for many people in positions of organizational authority is clear. They are being asked (and, in some cases, compelled) to share power with those they once regarded as their inferiors. From the viewpoint of many individual bosses who must make the change and live with its consequences, this presents a problem.

Institutions that have bred autocratic thinking and behavior shouldn't be shocked when their tyrannical offspring retreat, rather than charge ahead, when trumpets sound the call for worker empowerment. Professor C. K.

Prahalad, one of the world's foremost scholars of business organizations, implies that the end of these dictatorial work cultures may occur with more of a bang than a whimper. "You're telling top management that their accumulated intellectual capital is devalued," he writes, "that their thirty years of experience is less valuable as we move forward. This is so traumatic that senior managers [and I would add middle managers, supervisors, line foremen, and any other boss] find it hard to change unless there is a crisis."[5] Professor Prahalad is actually being optimistic. Crisis often causes bosses to regress into autocratic behavior rather than venture ahead, as he suggests, toward new, unfamiliar, more democratic territory.

Events at the Shelby Die Casting Company and at Bausch & Lomb's sunglasses plant illustrate some of the difficulty that organizational demands are creating for those in authority. In 1991, workers at Shelby Die were organized into teams and were named "associates." Despite training in group problem solving, a short while after the change occurred the teamwork evidently disintegrated. Associates and supervisors shouted and cursed at one another. Finally, the company's CEO simply cut the supervisory jobs. The results were one quarter of a million dollars in payroll savings, "associate" control of production with eventual productivity increases of 50 percent, and undoubtedly terror in the souls of every person of authority in an organization that was moving toward widespread participation, empowerment, and self-management.

In 1989, at Bausch & Lomb, 1,400 workers were organized into thirty-eight self-managed squads and managers received team-leader training. Within three years, half of these teams' managers had not worked out. The plant manager said, "I thought that it was a no-brainer. We spent a lot of time and money on professionals to teach motivation and leadership. But many people who were good soldiers under the old system just couldn't change."[6] Regardless of earlier success, managers lacking competence in newly demanded facilitator skills were reassigned.

Condemning these "old soldiers" seems to me to be unproductive. Bosses are us, after all, and change is difficult. It may be comforting for advocates of these changes to argue, "If they would only get on board, these old soldier/bosses will eventually have more power and influence, not less, after the changeover is completed, because subordinates will be less resistant and more forthcoming as they work in an atmosphere of cooperation, empowerment, and autonomy." But despite the validity of this line of reasoning, there is no reason to expect that it will convert a great many bosses, who have difficult tasks and nearby deadlines and autocratic habits, into instant, broad-minded "facilitators." Although worker empowerment and other nineties-style organizational changes may truly offer promise for the future, they are viewed as a handicap by many bosses who already feel overworked, overburdened, and overstressed. The work, burden, and stress were too great for Luis's and Terry's bosses, and perhaps also for many of the bosses at the Shelby Die Casting Company and Bausch & Lomb.

Pundits frequently attribute failures to introduce progressive organizational changes to such hindrances as poor planning, shortages of top management support, incompatible pay plans, inappropriate selection and orientation programs, and misaligned management information systems. At one time or another, these have probably all been factors in companies' inability to change, but it is evident that there is another major contributor: the abusive behavior of bosses who feel under siege. Feeling powerless, they enforce their power over others; feeling frightened, they explode, piling abuse on their frightened subordinates; feeling small, they belittle others in the futile hope that it will make them appear big.

THE EXECUTIONER

Relentless restructuring, for many of the world's organizations, is this decade's credo. Becoming "lean" is a commonly espoused corporate objective; consequently, it's only a few bosses who have not had firsthand experience with becoming executioners and laying off subordinates.

Consider the following abridged chronology of typical 1990s world events. A record was set at the outset of the decade when, between 1987 and 1993, 1.4 million executives, administrators, and managers lost their jobs.[7] That was not the end of the bad news. During the week of January 24, 1993, four of the country's leading corporations announced their intention to cut 100,000 jobs.[8] Six months later, Procter & Gamble issued a plan for a 12 percent workforce reduction. And in December, AT&T and Xerox announced that they would be making their moves toward "leanness" with job cuts amounting to as many as one-third of their employees. Secretary of Labor Robert Reich reported at the close of 1993 that in the last four months, American companies had cut jobs at the alarming rate of 2,000 per day, a 30 percent increase over the same period a year earlier.[9] And the new year's news was hardly less bleak: During the first quarter of 1994, Americans lost 3,100 jobs a day.[10]

Despite the occasional bit of favorable news about job growth, the problem continues. During the first quarter of 1995, for instance, in the face of *rising* profits, Mobil announced a one-third reduction in its Fairfax, Virginia, workforce. Similarly distressing news came from Boeing, another massive employer. "Lean" is in, and dismissals are commonplace in the United States and in other industrialized countries.

If you are throwing your hands skyward in exasperation, thinking that I don't know that payrolls sometimes bloat to unhealthy proportions, or suspecting that I'm a pie-in-the-sky softy who doesn't believe in firing employees, then bring them back down. After the decades I've spent analyzing organizations, I know that the unexpected occurs and that changing business conditions alter the levels of payroll burden that companies can bear. Dismissals are simply a fact of organizational life. However, they are also overused and overrated as a means of budget management. Only one-third of companies that downsize report gains in either customer service or productivity, and fewer than half say that they actually realized the growth they hoped for in their operating profits.[11] Furthermore, because of their cumulative effects on national spending and saving, dismissals may be a terribly counterproductive intervention from the perspective of society at large. Taxpayers plow about $22 billion into regular unemployment insurance benefits every year, and no wonder: In 1992, for instance, 21 percent of the unemployed hadn't worked in six months or longer, as compared with 11 percent in the 1970s and 15 percent in the eighties.[12] Nevertheless, the fact remains that from an individual company's perspective, there are times when dismissal emerges as the remedy of choice.

The resulting unemployment produces suffering for its victims and their families. Witness the 11 percent increase in mental health problems among the relatively affluent and educated residents of Dutchess County, New York, after IBM's layoffs,[13] then imagine the long-term human consequences of chronic unemployment for less advantaged regional and ethnic groups. Despite that suffering, there is nothing in the eight years of data I've collected that suggests that firing people, even large numbers of people, causes workers to feel automatically disrespected. My respondents recognized that being fired was materially and psychologically painful, but disrespect entered the picture only as a consequence of the manner in which the dismissals were handled. Kind, entirely painless ways to fire employees may not exist, but there are certainly some approaches to dismissal that are cruel and humiliating. The irony is that this cruelty helps the bosses who employ it to protect their self-images.

Personnel cuts produce pain in many bosses who wield the executioner's ax, and it is their efforts to avoid this pain that often produces abusive disrespect of subordinates. The discomfort occurs because bosses, being human and even humane, must find ways of reconciling a central contradiction: They are doing harmful things to people who do not deserve to be harmed. Have you noticed, for example, how little talk of "firing" there is in an era when it is all-too-commonplace? Instead, bosses and organizations use words like "downsize," "rightsize," "disemploy," or "RIFs (Reductions in Force)."

Why is such reconciliation necessary for bosses? The reason concerns matters that psychologists have investigated for quite some time.

DEHUMANIZERS, BLAMERS, AND RATIONALIZERS

Human beings prefer to think that the world is just, and will go to some length in order to maintain that view. Remarkably, research has shown that even when people suffer an actual accident—slipping on ice, a car crash—there is a tendency for others to perceive the victims as deserving their fates. Hence, the world remains a good and orderly place if the fate of those we fire or abuse at work is written off as a merited result of their own failures. Then we do not need to cope with incongruous thoughts such as *good people do cruel things* or *good people suffer needlessly.*

Three strategies help bosses to reconcile these contradictory concepts and preserve their own positive self-images. Unfortunately, all three result in bosses' ability to abuse subordinates, and even fire them, without the impediment of a guilty conscience.

Dehumanizers, one category of bosses, use a strategy that transforms their victims into nameless, faceless numbers. Diminishing their own awareness of victims' humanity helps the Dehumanizers to avoid a vivid sense of their suffering and their fate. Numbers do not have a history or future. They do not have families, tears, fears, or friends. With the individualizing details of victims erased from the foreground of bosses' imaginations, the lives of employees are not filled with day care, vacations, parents, and personal goals. Some companies have claimed that they do not have the internal talent to handle dismissals or the severe disciplining of staff, and they recruit "dirty-work specialists" from the outside. I think that this decision has less to do with talent than with psychology. For outsiders, a company's employees are more surely numbers. They share no history of jokes and quarrels. Outsiders look at numbers of people and make decisions uninhibited by any humane vision of their actions' consequences for people.

It's far more difficult for bosses to harm people whom they can envision worrying about kids' braces and parents' birthdays and who have dreams that are not too distant or different from their own. Thus, the Dehumanizers self-administer a kind of emotional anesthesia that diminishes their awareness of harm done, allowing them to act as tyrants and executioners without experiencing too much inhibitory, discomforting pain.

The events surrounding the American Airlines cabin attendants' strike that occurred in the autumn of 1993 seem to reflect the Dehumanizers' strategy. A front-page *New York Times* article reported: "It is not so much the pay or the benefits or sometimes the grinding four- and five-city, one-day trips or the interminable, unpaid delays between some flights. It is the little things that the striking flight attendants at American Airlines say grate on them and amount to a lack of respect."[14] Helen Neuhoff, a thirty-three-year-old flight attendant, said, "They treat us like we're disposable, a number." Another striker, Kylee Haviland, who had been on the job three years, said, "I'd rather be on the planes. But I've got to stand up for what I believe. My self-respect is more important than my job."[15] It is no problem for bosses to dismiss "just a number," and their lack of respect for workers as people shoves salt into the wounds opened by personal mistreatment and firings.

A second group of bosses, **Blamers,** protect their self-esteem by identifying the victims of layoff as *deserving victims.* The victims' deeds at work and their fate—either the suffering of abuse or unemployment—are contrived by Blamers as a perfect match.

An illustrative example of the Blamers' strategy is found in everyday life, when romantic partners, children, and parents must say good-bye to each other. Have you ever noticed how, on these occasions, people often bicker? They bicker because they feel badly about parting, because fighting reduces the pain of leave-taking by supporting the temporary illusion that staying together would not actually be so pleasant. Analogously, fighting with subordinates can serve to support the illusion that disrespectful treatment of them is deserved and that dismissals serve to rid the company of less worthy employees who shouldn't be there anyway. For bosses, finding a reason to be at odds with a worker is the easy part—subordinates are never perfect. Workers, in turn, often respond to bosses' lack of respect in ways that allow the bosses to judge that victimization of the workers would be justified, beginning a cycle that ultimately makes abuse and/or unjust firing easier. *After all,* the boss thinks, *clearly, this employee has not succeeded in earning my respect.*

Sloan, an associate producer in the television industry, had earned verbal and written accolades for her work. But when she was being fired in a sudden, across-the-board downsizing, her boss alleged that Sloan's achievements "weren't all your doing. A lot was attributable to your people." When Sloan diplomatically suggested that the performance of others, while laudable, reflected at least in part her guidance, her boss closed the case: "Well, looking back," she remarked, "no one thinks that they amount to as much as they seemed to at the time." Sloan recognized her boss as a Blamer. "She knew that I was good," Sloan said, "and that she had to get rid of me, and she just couldn't live with that. It was easier for her to think of me as incompetent."

The third group, the **Rationalizers,** manage feelings which might damage their self-image by fanatically embracing the idea that the few must be sacrificed for the good of the many. This line of thinking justifies—and rewards—bosses who can be ruthless in their treatment of workers or in the trimming of payrolls in order to *get the job done.* Unless leaders possess the necessary severity, Rationalizers warn us, our competitors will eat us, and the company, for lunch.

In 1993 *The Wall Street Journal* carried a front-page story about Jack the Ripper.[16] The Ripper is actually John F. Grundhoffer, chairman of First Bank Systems, whose specialties apparently include firing people. In three years he dismissed 2,000 employees, a full 20 percent of his organization's workforce. Subsequently, net income climbed, pleasing investors, who traded the company's share price to nearly double its original value. (Of course, cutting payroll costs commonly increases net income in the short term, which investors like, but their likelihood of producing long-term benefits and growth is not very great. Statistics suggest that fewer than half of the companies that significantly cut their workforces actually realize noteworthy gains.)[17] Mr. Grundhoffer himself appears not to have been totally unaffected by the firings, but he went ahead anyway, stating, "It's for the greater good." Many bosses who abuse or fire employees find it necessary to fortify themselves before, during, and afterward with claims about their courage in doing *the right thing* for the company despite their own regret and loneliness and the short-term pain it causes for a few workers.

The Rationalizers often assert that once a boss has decided that discipline or dismissal is the appropriate course of action, it should be done swiftly and without consideration of individuals. After all, these bosses are acting on behalf of the greater good. True to this school of thought, the Grundhoffer firings were reportedly done swiftly, in mass-execution style. Employees were told to be at a certain worksite at 8 A.M. Once they were assembled, they were informed that they were being fired and the severance package was explained. The greater good was served, and, as in other examples of disrespect by Dehumanizers, Blamers, and Rationalizers, the suffering experienced by victims was needlessly multiplied.

THE DIVINE RIGHT OF ABUSERS

Until this point, this chapter has concerned itself with the 1990s work environment and its capacity to be a breeding ground for abuse by bosses. This, the chapter's final section, turns to a powerful cause of worker abuse that is reason for alarm because it is both ancient and modern. It concerns divine right, "cream rising to the top," and *The Concise Oxford Dictionary* definition of "subordinate": "Of inferior importance or rank; second-ary; subservient."[18] Organizational hierarchies steer some bosses toward thinking and behaving as if a "boss" were truly *superior* and a subordinate truly *inferior*.

Nathan, who would become one of the highest execu-tives in his *Fortune* top-ten company, was already occu-pying a senior position in one of the company's major divisions when he told me his story.

We were reviewing business performance in Scandina-via. Thirty or forty people were at the meeting. Presenta-tions were being given, and the head of the conference, the "big boss," was attacking the presentation of the Scandinavian group. What he was saying was not right. He was raising his voice and everyone was cowering. I felt vulnerable and tried to keep my mouth shut. Then I heard a voice, my own, disagreeing with his facts. I knew the situation since I had just been there and had done the study, and he didn't have it right—it wasn't a matter of opinion.

The boss leaned back and looked at me. "I don't care about your position," he said. "You have no right to speak." My immediate superior kicked me to be quiet. The big boss wanted me to kill the study, to lie, misrepre-sent, be inauthentic. I would have had no integrity. He believed that subordinates had no right to engage in free thought. He had actually said that to others: Disagree-ment was disrespect. If you were a rung below, you were lesser. Obedience, not judgment, was required. Your duty was to be obedient and loyal. "L'état, c'est moi. Obedi-ence to me is God's will, and the will of nature."

Disrespect of subordinates is not an inevitable consequence of spending an adult lifetime in an organization's hierarchy, but it is a natural and common one. Hierarchies advance the breeding of subordinate-abusing bosses by providing symbols of separateness that encourage a sense of superiority. Occupying an upper rung in an organization's ladder invites some bosses to believe that their position is a reflection of personal advantages that go beyond work-related talent to inherent individual superiority.

When the ladder's steps correspond to large differences in privilege, it makes matters worse. Those with obvious perks and signs of prestige are even more encouraged to act as if they are an elite class and deserve to be one. They think nothing of having precious air cargo space in corporate jets filled with their favorite bottled water (a true story) or ordering underlings to retrieve jewelry that was swallowed by an elephant (also true). When these bosses commit the Eight Daily Sins—Deceit, Constraint, Coercion, Selfishness, Inequity, Cruelty, Disregard, and Deification—their violations do not arise out of a defense of their self-image, nor are they unfortunate impulses driven by pressures of stress and vulnerability. For these Brahmin, abusive disrespect of subordinates is a permissible and appropriate expression of personal privilege.

What others experience as mistreatment by these bosses, the bosses experience as unobjectionable and even necessary. Civil treatment of others who are not of the elite class is not required. Others are objects, instruments to suit the needs of superiors, and are not equivalently human—if they were, they would possess rights that constrain bosses' behavior. Abusive disrespect signals the abuser's views of subordinates as inferior people in the same way that some people's treatment of service personnel, calling them by their first names (or "girl," "girly," "boy," and so on) while expecting to be addressed by them as something loftier ("sir," "madam," and the like), signals social superiority. Such abuse represents not only obedience to a stated hierarchy but an eagerness to enforce the relationship's asymmetry.

Japanese unions prevent the growth of privileges that would encourage one worker to believe that he or she has more dignity or worth than another. If an employee at the organizational ladder's bottom has to wear a company jacket and punch in, then so do other employees, whatever their position. Holidays, medical care, and seniority rules are uniform—and it has become cliché to write about comparative pay ratios, smaller in Japan than in most of the rest of the world. In the United States, for example, executives receive 50 to 100 times the pay of hourly workers; in Japan, the ratio is about 10 to 1.[19]

Are boss-subordinate relations more harmonious in Japan than in the United States or elsewhere? There are no data that provide certain proof of that conclusion, but stories and studies comparing Japanese management practices with what goes on in the rest of the world suggest that it is very likely the case. And if it is true that such differences in on-the-job respect exist, then it follows that the hierarchical differences in privilege both reflect and contribute to differences in levels of civility.

Differences in privilege concern distributions of wealth, and thus are a matter for economists and ethicists to ponder. My concern is with the impact of vastly unequal privilege on self and social perception at the workplace. Large, ostensible differences in supposed status diminish the view that all employees, bosses and subordinates, hourlies and executives, are fundamentally equal members of the same community, possessing the same dignity and worth, with entitlements to fair treatment and respect at work that are absolutely indistinguishable.

Look around and you will find examples of organizational Darwinism, the concept that some—i.e., bosses—are inherently more fit to rule, thrive, and survive. It is evident in who is comfortable addressing whom by first name, in the allocation of parking places, in access to dining rooms. Watch who goes through doors first and listen to the excuses bosses give for their oppression of subordinates: *They only work for the money and are not as trustworthy as we are . . . or as hardworking . . . or as able to handle bad news . . . or* _____. (You fill in the blank.)

Hierarchy lends itself to the breeding of elitist thinking about self and others, but such thinking is not the invariable outcome of hierarchy. Great numbers of bosses are seduced into embracing an ideology of superiority, but many escape it. Unfortunately, its seductive powers seem greater in times like these, the 1990s, when bosses are feeling especially under the gun and are seeking means to shore up their sagging egos.

For some bosses, of course, the appeal of such an ideology is constantly great, regardless of work conditions or the state of the market. Their hopes, dreams, fears, and fantasies thrive on a diet of abusing the weak. Their stories are the subject of this book's next chapter.

CHAPTER THREE

ABUSE FOR ITS OWN SAKE:

Bred to Bully

Steve Jobs of Apple Computer fame, now the entrepreneurial force behind Next Computer, has at least one more distinction to his credit: In 1993, he was identified as one of America's most difficult bosses.[1] On the occasion of this black-humored award, several stories about Mr. Job's treatment of subordinates were offered as evidence of his merit. One of these was about an exchange that began when he was told by a manager that the cost to produce a computer's external casing would be $200. Mr. Jobs declared that the amount was $180 too much and berated the manager with a curse-filled, four-minute tirade.

Juan Trippe, the founder of Pan Am, also holds membership in the legion of "bosses from hell." Descriptions characterize Mr. Trippe as capricious and mean-spirited, a boss who reportedly fired subordinates simply because they bothered him. His legacy, some claim, was an airline unprepared for deregulation.[2]

Charles Bluhorn, who grew Gulf and Western from a modest auto-parts company into a giant multinational corporation, has also been nominated to the bullying bosses hall of fame. He was known to go into foaming-at-the-mouth rages, denigrate subordinates, and demand personal favors.[3]

Neither you nor I can fully know what motivates the behavior of bosses like these three. Explanations of bosses' behavior that rely on speculation about the inner workings of the mind run the risk of becoming psychobabble. Exploring why any particular boss abuses employees on any particular occasion is, at best, an enterprise of considerable uncertainty. It is also an enterprise that, at the very least, requires in-depth information from the boss him- or herself. Nonetheless, the subordinate abuse of Jobs, Trippe, Bluhorn, and many other bosses whose stories are shared in this chapter are useful vehicles for illustrating a class of boss behavior that is as dangerous as it is distinct from the ones discussed in the last chapter.

Rather than a toxic effect of external and organizational circumstances, a significant amount of abusive boss behavior is the result of enduring, malignant forces that exist inside the bosses themselves. Data from working men and women across the country indicate that more than 10 percent of all bosses indulge in such gratuitous abuse. When sheer malevolence is responsible for the active disrespect of subordinates, it has nothing to do with uncontrollable explosion ignited by job-related stress. Instead, this abuse represents bosses' self-serving efforts to enhance their own feelings of power, competence, and value at subordinates' expense. The differences between the two types of abuse are not all that subtle, and are easily recognized by victimized subordinates who see clear distinctions in the context, frequency, and purpose of the mistreatment.

When malignant, internal motives are responsible for bosses' misbehavior, the abusive acts exhibit an unceasing regularity that is not obviously calibrated to the peaks and valleys of organizational circumstance. The reason for this relentlessness is frequently obvious and frightening to subordinates: The cruel disrespect of workers that is born of bosses' characters has no reason or purpose other than the act of abuse itself. It is not a cathartic outburst produced by tension, nor is its goal the prevention of some real or imagined organizational adversity. This is abuse for the sake of abuse. Malignantly motivated bosses experience temporary relief, and sometimes even ghastly pleasure, because they have diminished another human being's sense of power, competence, or self-worth. And those sick gains simply whet their appetite for the next go-round.

For clarity's sake, I will describe and categorize malignantly motivated bosses as falling into three groups, here labeled Conquerors, Performers, and Manipulators. Reality, of course, is messier than this, as evidenced by the real-life stories that are shared throughout the chapter. Bosses often combine traits from two or three of the categories, and many personalities resist such all-encompassing labels. Nonetheless, any worker will recognize bosses past and present in these three departments, and bosses

—if they are so honest—may well catch a glimpse of themselves.

The **Conqueror**'s world is a matter of power and turf. Since for Conquerors bigger is always better, and winning occurs only when another loses, their hunger to defeat and humiliate others is insatiable. Conquerors *bludgeon* subordinates.

Performers fret constantly about their own competence. Unfortunately for them and their subordinates, the lofty standards of ability that they pursue are often unattainable. Consequently, in an effort to boost their perpetually sagging self-estimates, Performers *belittle* subordinates and, as a result, feel (temporarily) more able.

Manipulators wonder obsessively about others' views of their worth. Approval, particularly from superiors, is all that Manipulators really care about, and is always—in their eyes—in great demand and short supply. Manipulators work with greed and cunning to bolster their reputations by making others appear unworthy. Their signature strategy is to *betray* subordinates.

Bosses falling into each of these three categories possess distinguishing motives, a preferred weapon with which to abuse subordinates, and a worldview that both stimulates and justifies the weapon's use. Knowing about these malignantly motivated bosses can be beneficial to your health. For that reason, what follows is an account of who they are, what they do, and why they do it.

CONQUERORS

Linda Wachner, CEO of Warnaco, has increased the company's stockholders' equity by well over $100 million. She is also reputed to be a bona fide bully. Once she exploded at a meeting of executives from the women's clothing department. Furious at their performance, she announced, "You're eunuchs. How can your wives stand you? You've got nothing between your legs!"[4] On another occasion, Ms. Wachner supposedly told a new company president to fire some people so that his employees would respect him. The intended message illustrates both the self-doubt that dwells within Conquerors and the reason bludgeoning is their preferred weapon for relieving that doubt: It makes others less powerful and makes the wielder seem a force to be taken seriously.

Conquerors bludgeon because bludgeoning puts them in control. This group of bosses thrives on the feeling of power they derive from subjugating others to their wishes and whims.

Kent worked in a retail clothing company. A boss two levels above, whose abuse Kent and his fellow workers suffered regularly, is still employed by the company.

The boss called to inquire why we were over budget for the month. When I tried to explain, he interrupted, saying that the bottom line was that "it had better not happen again." He then hung up the phone in my face, and called two other managers into his office about the bud-

get overage on their day off. He cursed at them and
yelled, once more, that it had better not happen again.

All these abuses happened regularly, Kent explained, in the absence of any real crisis, and without any enduring or productive consequence. In fact, the opposite occurred: People quit and engaged in subterfuge in order to avoid the boss's mistreatment. But for Kent's boss, the pleasure obviously lay in his power to hang up in people's faces, call them curse words, order their presence at work on vacation days, and warn them repeatedly and condescendingly that behaviors that displeased him "had better not happen again." Organizationally unproductive outcomes can have little impact on someone who enjoys more than anything the bludgeoning itself.

Two employees, complete strangers to each other, independently characterized the same media company by invoking images of the former Soviet dictator Joseph Stalin. Celeste said, "It was a Stalinist nightmare." As she described them, her colleagues were in misery, spending much of their time on internal politics and on attempts to destroy one another. She blamed her boss—a Conqueror —for these nightmarish conditions. "She created an atmosphere of complete paranoia, and seemed to enjoy the outcomes. She was dour and secretive and appeared wired as if she could explode at any time."

Conquerors do not have to do their own bludgeoning in order to experience pleasure. Their need to feel powerful and in control is just as easily satisfied when they can sit and watch subordinates disembowel one another in battles they've arranged. Stalin had a sadistic predilection for arbitrarily arresting the wives and children of his underlings, and then watching the bereft husbands fearfully obey his bidding in the hopes of a release from prison. As arbitrarily as he'd commanded the arrest, Stalin would order the release, demonstrating the extent to which, like other Conquerors, he relished the absolute control and subjugation of other human beings. In the same way, Celeste's boss held the power of occupational life or death for subordinates. She, not they, determined who would battle and who would emerge as the victor. Stalin's methods were more horrifying and his aspirations larger in scale, but his motives overlap with those of Conquerors in today's workplaces, who are empowered by their ability to disempower others.

PERFORMERS

Performers are certain of their abilities only when they put down the abilities of their charges. Humiliating, degrading, and frequently public assaults are Performers' weapons of choice. Subordinates lacking the capacity to retaliate are their favorite targets. When Performers belittle subordinates, they perceive their own skills as enlarged by comparison. For Performers, the experience is addictive, as it overcomes doubts they have about their own talent—but only momentarily.

Another story about Steve Jobs indicates that he may be designated a Performer. Apparently, two engineers from his Next Company failed to design successfully a computer chip by a preset deadline, despite fifteen months of hard work, including weekends and holidays. Of course, delays happen—but not without consequence if you work for Steve Jobs, who "publicly and viciously berated them before the entire company for not working faster."[5]

Hard-nosed skeptics may argue that when bosses behave as Mr. Jobs did, it's merely functional. A common contention is that they're putting the fear of God into subordinates, letting witnesses know that unless they deliver, the same belittling is in store for them. Bosses don't really mean it personally, these skeptics might say, nor do they really take personally the shortcomings of employees.

Not so, I'm afraid. Performers belittle because it makes them feel good, not because it's good for employee motivation or organizational performance. As evidence, one of the two Next engineers who were publicly abused quit right after the project was finished. In addition, employees of Mr. Jobs say they sometimes submit their worst work to him first, before turning in their best, because they know that he automatically rejects what he sees first. This is certainly inefficient from a business perspective, yet it is productive from a personal one: By anticipating the thoughtless rejection, employees avoid being put down for the work in which they have the greatest pride and most investment. In the decades that I've served as a management educator and organizational consultant, the fear of God has shown no benefits beyond a perverse thrill for the one dishing it out.

Richard has impressive credentials. He earned both his undergraduate and master's degrees in engineering, and has an MBA from an Ivy League business school. His employer builds airplanes. Richard told me about his boss, a man who regularly humiliated his subordinates in public and private.

His targets were usually those of us who were most competent, which is really what made the whole thing so weird. I mean, if you're really concerned about performance you don't pick on those who are performing best. But to him it seemed as if nothing anyone did was enough. If you did well, it could always have been better. What he'd get you for, a lot of the time, were not the big things. It was for small infractions, slight oscillations from the standard.

One of my peers turned in a report which we all had a hand in developing. There was a form that reports were supposed to have which other groups regularly modified as the need arose. She'd done so, and the contents of this particular report were good. She had done a nice job integrating some difficult material, and there was plenty of time to revise, if necessary. But the boss went into one of his things. You never knew when it was coming. He said something like "There are ways of organizing reports which you do not have the knowledge or skill to judge or change." Really talking down to her in our presence. Telling her how awful her performance was, which it wasn't. "There is right and wrong and you don't seem able to do it right," he said.

Upset by the real and imagined imperfections that they sense in themselves, Performers like Richard's boss find perverse comfort in raging at the real and imagined imperfections of others, as minor and inconsequential as they might be. Doing so diminishes the qualities of employees to whom they might be compared and deflects attention from the deficiencies that they fear they possess.

MANIPULATORS

"Self-centered," "selfish," "untrustworthy," and "narcissistic" are words that workers commonly use when characterizing bosses who are Manipulators. What counts for Manipulators are their own needs, feelings, thoughts, belongings, and reputations. Everybody and everything else is secondary. If subordinates count at all in Manipulators' eyes, it is only in that they can be instrumental in helping the Manipulators gain approval and avoid disapproval.

Behavior that subordinates may experience as mistreatment by Manipulators, Manipulators themselves experience as entirely acceptable, if not essential. Universal social rules requiring the decent treatment of others do not influence Manipulators' behavior, since subordinates are largely regarded by them not as people but as objects and instruments. Objects and instruments cannot be abused; they can only be used effectively—or else be useless.

Julie's boss regularly used subordinates to advance her own standing in the company.

My manager was insecure in her position. In a strategy to make herself look better to other bosses, she took most of the credit when projects were successful, and was the first to place blame when they were not. On one occasion, she announced to our entire group of eight managers that she was assigning my project to one of my peers. This announcement was made publicly, without any ad-

*vance consultation with me. I asked her about the move
privately after the meeting, and she claimed it wasn't her
decision but her manager's call. I paid a visit to her manager to present my point of view. Her manager claimed
she not only did not make the decision but advised
against it. What a coward my manager was! She was only
concerned about acceptance of her and her own personal
gain.*

From another respondent who also had a boss with a
reputation for betrayal, lying, and deception comes a report of equally insidious treatment.

*I had been away from my service rep job for the phone
company for nine months, and when I returned, I worked
for a supervisor I had not known before I left. I was frustrated getting back to the previous level of my skills and
knowledge, and after the second week back at my job, at
the end of a long, busy day, I started to cry. My supervisor took me aside and I shared my frustration with her.
She listened as I explained that my upset state was
caused by my inability to recall all the procedures, forms,
and so on. She assured me that I would get it all back in
due time, and that was the end of our chat.*

*Our office moved three months later and I was reas-
signed to another supervisor. My new supervisor asked
me if I was familiar with all the write-ups in my performance binder. I told her "yes," but I was wrong. I was
shocked to find a write-up of my frustrated chat months
earlier that stated that I was "angry" and demonstrated a
"poor attitude." The write-up totally misrepresented our
discussion, my performance, and my attitude. It turns
out my previous supervisor's reputation was one of*

sneaky tactics. She apparently was incapable of being up front with people.

As these stories make plain, another telltale attribute of Manipulators is that they are easily threatened. And it is no wonder. In their single-minded pursuit of approval, they make themselves vulnerable to any hint of disapproval. Subordinates unwittingly slight Manipulators when they miss or show up late for meetings, regardless of the reason. If subordinates suggest additions or alternatives to a Manipulator's ideas, even when that boss has invited them to do so, there is a good chance that this will be seen as disapproval of the ideas, and in return the worker runs the risk of becoming a target of a Manipulator's vengeful, abusive disrespect.

Sources report that their bosses' responses at these times are punctuated by comments that make it clear that they are not offering remedial reprimand for faulty work performance; they are issuing punishment for not showing complete and unadulterated approval. Employees also report feeling that once they are targeted by Manipulators as having questioned the worth of their superiors, they will never be forgiven. Instead, they will remain the target of their bosses' abuse, disproportionate to any possible work-related misdeed, forevermore.

Manipulators require constant approbation; anything less strikes at their harbored self-doubt and questions concerning their real value. Consequently, Manipulators work hard to control the performance feedback they are given. One way they do so is by becoming *abdicrats*. Abdicrats can be recognized by their cunning use of their own absence as a managerial tool. One respondent complained of his boss, "The guy was never around. He would hide away, then pop out and chew us out for not doing what he wanted. But, hell, how the heck were we supposed to know what he wanted? We would only get a passing word here or there, or an EM, or a Post-it on your door or desk.''

Manipulators practicing abdicracy never quite state their opinions or assignments, since such a commitment risks evaluation and disapproval. Instead of declaring, they waffle, dancing to and fro on the periphery of an issue, until the matter's success or failure becomes clear. Then Manipulators launch their betrayal, claiming successes as their own and blaming subordinates for whatever failures may have occurred.

In fact, respondents' disclosures lead me to believe that each of the three malignantly motivated boss types have their own breed of abdicrat. Conquerors occasionally take a turn as abdicrats because the ambiguity it creates forces subordinates into greater dependency, as they fearfully struggle to learn what it will take to avoid the Conquerors' bludgeoning. Performers sometimes use abdicracy as a means of filling subordinates with confusion and caution, two ingredients sure to erode subordinate competence and confidence and thus produce the raw material for Performers' belittling. And Manipulators choose to be abdicrats because, at the day's end, it allows them to join the winning side, unfettered by any previous declaration about where they truly stand on an issue.

On the surface, the three malevolent boss types may seem different, but scratch the surface and they are not dissimilar. For all three, the core issue is an aggravating personal question that reflects their own special brand of self-doubt. Conquerors wonder, *Am I powerful?* Performers ask themselves, *Am I competent?* And Manipulators worry, *Am I valued?* In their flailing efforts to quell self-doubts, all three, when dealing with subordinates, seem contemptuous of ordinary person-to-person rules. Their primary criterion for choosing one action over another is a judgment of the action's capacity to produce the sense of power, competence, or value for which they hunger. Unfortunately for these bosses, and for their staffs as well, their hunger cannot be satisfied.

THE EXCEPTIONS

Examples of bosses who are not motivated by cruelty demonstrate that more just and open-minded organizational leaders exist—and succeed. For example, Mike Husar, a plant manager at a GM auto components manufacturing site, achieved notable production increases by creating a culture in which employees worked cooperatively in order to improve their work effectiveness.[6] One assembly-line worker was quoted as saying that the management "actually listened to what we had to say, and made you feel like there was more cooperation. And it's working."

It's also working, without any bludgeoning, belittling, or betraying, at Lotus Development Corporation. Evidence comes from a story about June L. Rokoff, *a.k.a.* St. June, or the Iron Lady, a senior vice-president for software development. Just one of Ms. Rokoff's successes was the release of Lotus's spreadsheet for DOS called Release 3. The project was in trouble and she saved it not by being abusive but by creating trust and commitment among the programmers and technologists reporting to her.[7] The workers say that she created a healthy climate by performing the essential tasks of a competent leader— identifying clear objectives, developing a means of communicating them, setting up short-term checkpoints for indexing progress toward longer-term goals, and running efficient problem-solving meetings—as well as by attending to her work group's socio-emotional needs. At her initiative, special steps were undertaken to publicly acknowledge employees' individual and collective achievements. Late-night work was rewarded with a gourmet meal prepared by Lotus executives. A series of events directed effort at building team members' work relationships. June L. Rokoff is an extremely competent boss not because she abuses subordinates but because she fosters cooperation.

Lawrence Gladstone is also impressive, able but not cruel in his management of subordinates. Mr. Gladstone is president of Sequins International, a $30 million-a-year company located in the New York City borough of Queens. Prior to launching his initiatives, according to Mr. Gladstone, the company "operated with a whip-and-stick approach, with supervisors and bean counters. The human beings were broken down,"[8] a treatment not uncommon in the garment industry. Competition from other low-cost producers is keen, and in parts of the United States many garment industry employees are non-English-speaking, uneducated members of our society's most disadvantaged groups. Sequin International's 350 employees do not seem to be an exception. Mr. Gladstone decided that it was more profitable to build people up than to break them down. Workers, now operating in teams, have the opportunity to shape their working conditions; they are given assistance in handling social and physical problems; and, during work time, the company provides for the teaching of English as a second language. Mr. Gladstone, who claims that his decisions were guided more by economic reality than by altruism, evidently made the right choices. Since his initiatives were implemented, production efficiency has improved 80 percent.

Bosses like Mike Husar, June Rokoff, and Lawrence Gladstone succeed by raising subordinates' dignity, not by lowering it. Instead of using subordinates as objects to meet their own needs, bosses like these three work with subordinates in order to achieve organizational goals. They invite subordinate participation and treat contrary ideas coming from subordinates as fundamental raw material for organizational improvement, not as personal challenges to their self-aggrandizement.

Malignantly motivated bosses indulge in the opposite behavior. For them, the disparate suggestions and independent ideas of employees are declarations of war. They see their power, competence, and value as under constant attack. Regardless of business conditions and events, the matter is always personal, rarely benign, and usually deserving, as they see it, of an abusive response. If you were to meet such a person on the street, in a store, or at a social event, you would either avoid them or, perhaps with the help of others, set them straight. But workers usually lack safe access to such options. Scarce job markets, bosses' control over employees' fates, and personal financial obligations put a de facto end to freedoms that exist outside of work. In short, you've got to take it.

An agitated young man had just described his abuse by

a mean-spirited boss, and was rapidly clasping and unclasping his hands.

What could I do? Sometimes you can appeal to higher-ups, but not always. Not this time. It's a political game and bosses have their superiors' ears, if you know what I mean. You've got to take it. I mean, you feel like hell—a fool, a child. Forget sleeping or eating. But what can you do? You suffer.

Whether at the hands of bosses who are themselves under the gun, or by superiors who abuse for the sake of it, victimized subordinates suffer. They are harmed in body, mind, spirit, and their ability to work.

CHAPTER FOUR

THE ABUSED:

Well-Being and Work Performance

I'm a schoolteacher, and have been for quite a while. My job has had its problems, of course—children can be difficult, and there are problems of dealing with parents, lack of resources, weekend and evening commitments—but I always enjoyed going to work. All that changed six years ago.

The principal was new to the school but not to the job. It was his first year with us. We knew that he had a reputation for being autocratic and dictatorial. Anyway, because of my specific responsibilities at the time and my professional background, I had an obligation to join in a discussion of an issue that came up. There was a half day of meetings where I raised a number of questions and generally offered the best advice that I could. My participation in the discussions evidently upset the principal. I knew that one day later.

Following my regular routine, I left my classroom and turned into a back corridor to use a stairway that provided convenient access to a lower floor and the teachers' lounge. I'd spend a few moments in the lounge during this period, just to unwind, then I'd return to the room to do whatever the day's chores might be. As I descended the stairs, the principal and one of his cronies were approaching from the opposite direction. I thought nothing of their approach until he, the principal, blocked my way. His friend walked up a step or two until he was situated behind me.

I said, "Hello, Dr. Blank. Excuse me."

He mimicked, "Hello, Dr. Blank. Excuse me."

I tried to step around him, but he moved with me and then moved up to the step just below the one that I stood on, breathing in my face.

I said, "I'd like to go by, please," or something of the sort. He mimicked me again. He said something like "If you ever interfere with my command again, you'll find walking anywhere in this school system difficult."

I turned to walk back upstairs and this other person blocked my way. I'm a small woman and both of them were large men. Finally I said, "Excuse me, or I will shout for help." Perhaps I should have said that sooner, or perhaps I should have simply shouted without warning, but I didn't. It's hard to keep one's wits at times like those. He opened the path and said that he didn't want to hear from me again about this episode or anything else, or else there would be trouble.

I was shaking. They were serious, I'm sure. I thought of telling others or writing a letter, but there was no proof, and they said that I would be accused of trying to create trouble by lying. I'm a private person, not married, and I was very frightened—even more so afterward than during. A lot changed after that. I was traumatized. Although I have since changed schools, the event stays with me. Honestly, since that time I have been ill at ease and distracted, and much less relaxed in the classroom. Every strain seems so much greater. My confidence was permanently shaken. They stole something very dear to me.

Since then, the principal has become a prominent figure in the state's educational establishment.

Bosses can make or break your day, your month, your year, your career. They have the power to ease or intensify adverse reactions to normal organizational stress. Empirical evidence broadcasts a consistent message: People reporting to more considerate bosses are less likely to suffer the ravages of burnout and more likely to experience work satisfaction than those reporting to less considerate bosses. In fact, as an inoculation against burnout, respect from a boss offers more protection than salary. Conversely, there is solid evidence that working for unsupportive bosses is associated with higher levels of anxiety, depression, and even heart disease.[1]

Data collected by the United Health Care Corporation support this distressing link between unhappy work environments and unhealthy workers. Of the 1,000 employees surveyed, 28 percent of those from the northeastern United States and 15 percent of those from the western United States reported stress reactions—sleep disturbances, headaches, stomach disorders—that they attributed to disrespectful treatment by bosses.[2]

By placing emphasis on bosses' behavior as a determi-

nant of subordinate well-being, I have no desire to obscure the obvious: Peer support and lack thereof, as well
as the pace and pattern of business, certainly have many
of the same personal consequences as boss behavior.
However, an accumulating body of evidence identifies
relations with bosses as the factor that has the strongest
impact on employees' well-being.[3] And if *unsupportive*
and *inconsiderate* bosses are detrimental to workers'
health and psychology, then think of the personal havoc
wreaked—among an estimated 90-plus percent of employees—by bosses who are outright *abusive.*

Margaret's story provides an example.

*It was Monday morning, and we were in the middle of
a meeting with a number of people from both our staffs.
All of a sudden my boss smiled and ordered me to get her
a cup of coffee, specifying cream, sugar, and so on.
"What an odd request," I thought to myself, but the
smile, which in retrospect seems more of a smirk, made
me think that it was a joke. After all, I was a vice-president, earning about $120,000 a year. She had to be teas-
ing. So I smiled back and said, "If you really want one,
I'll ask Martha [a secretary] to take the orders."*

*"No," she said. "You get it." She pointed her finger
directly at me, a few inches from my face. I was flabber-
gasted. She had picked on me in the past but not like
this, and not in public, although I'd seen her do so to
others.* But I am a top performer, *I always said to myself.*
She'd never do it to me.

*I was angry and humiliated. In order to win back some
of my rapidly eroding self-respect, I knew that I should
say something, but I didn't feel safe saying anything. So I
got up and delivered her coffee, and then sat there in a*

*pool of perspiration, with my heart racing and the begin-
nings of a pounding headache, which lasted for days—
surprise, surprise.*

Abusive disrespect is always unpleasant, no matter the
source or setting. It always threatens its victim's sense of
self-worth and well-being. But at work, when bosses mistreat subordinates, there are special dangers. Subordinates' dependency, because of bosses' power, market
conditions, and personal circumstances, often compel
them to endure the painful humiliation by suffering in
silence.

SUFFERING IN SILENCE

"How does humiliation make you feel?" considered a
personnel professional with whom I spoke. "Like there
are tears which will never stop. You retch in frustration
about what was done to you, about what happened,
about what it makes you, and in disgust about what
you're doing to yourself. Mostly, you can see the consequences of humiliation in victims' faces: masklike, without definition. The faces of beaten people suffering battle
fatigue."

A recent television advertisement for Federal Express
is appealing because it captures what many of us would
like to do to abusive bosses. The scene opens with a boss
entering a public work area shouting questions at his assistant, a young woman, about the whereabouts of a
package. Work stops as everyone is caught up in the tension of this dangerous exchange. With Federal Express

electronic information systems at her fingertips, the assistant easily locates the package and calmly gives the information to her menacing boss. Disarmed, he shuffles back to the interior of his office, whereupon everyone in the work area breaks into spontaneous cheering and applause. The assistant shares with them a broad smile of victory.

Subordinates who suffer bosses' abuse are treated as if they were second-class citizens, *nobodies* whose human rights are less than their bosses'. Understanding this dynamic is crucial to understanding why the consequences of cruel disrespect by bosses are so devastating. At the core of all oppressive behavior is a negation of another person's social worth. But at work, where any refutation of that negation is often constrained, the effects of abuse are multiplied.

When it happens outside the workplace, abusive disrespect can be met with either a demand for respectful treatment, a retort in kind, or a simple withdrawal from the scene. It is only very occasionally that the same options exist at work.

Thomas, a key executive in a *Fortune* top-fifty company, was responsible for managing a company move. He'd been abused—yelled at, flagrantly insulted—by his boss, who felt that a delay in readying his office was a personal slight. On one occasion Thomas stood up to the assault of his superior. But, as he explained it, special circumstances permitted him to do so and thereby avoid silent suffering.

I was sweating. I didn't want to get others in trouble. But suddenly I turned and started questioning him. "Where did you get your information from?" I asked.

"Why not speak to me first?" "Why not give me the cour-
tesy of a conversation?"

The truth is that I wouldn't have done that five, ten, or
twenty-five years earlier. Back then, I was a good soldier.
But now I was getting out of the business. They needed
me more than I needed them. Frankly, I wasn't brave, I
was just less vulnerable.

Sadly, the data suggest that this event is far from typical. Thomas's boldness is the exception. Usually subordinates are thoroughly vulnerable. They are trapped
because they need the job and because their bosses have
the power to make their lives miserable. Instead of demanding respect or walking out, they find themselves
limited to enduring the humiliation of boss abuse in silence, which takes its ultimate toll on their well-being.

I was assigned to a project by a senior employee. But
my immediate boss wanted me to continue on my current
job. Suddenly, a meeting was called, and my boss said to
me publicly, "Do what I say or you'll be fired." I thought
that he was kidding at first, but he wasn't. It was coercion
and I was the pawn. It was evident to everyone that this
was a way for him to get at this other very powerful per-
son. He was using me to get at him. My boss had no
respect for me.

After this I had trouble falling asleep. If I got up to go
to the bathroom, forget it, I could not get back to sleep. It
would go through my mind over and over: the scene,
what had been said, what I should have said—Forget it!
Take the money and position and shove it—but couldn't
afford to say.

HEALTH CONSEQUENCES

Decades of psychological and psychiatric research evidence has confirmed everyday experience and common sense by demonstrating that individual well-being is affected by the quality of social interaction at work. Employees who experience the work environment as cohesive, friendly, respectful, and supportive are less likely to show signs of depression or anxiety. When bosses' behaviors are entered into the equation of employee work experience, the impact on well-being is even greater.[4]

Please take a minute to complete the questionnaire that is included at the end of this book. Many hundreds of working men and women already have. Their scores, which are measures of their experiences of boss abuse, were correlated with their scores on three standard psychological assessment tests measuring depression, anxiety, and self-esteem. The results were straightforward and upsetting. Being subjected to a boss's abusive disrespect was clearly linked to adverse psychological states. Subordinates who were victims of mistreatment at work exhibited more depression and anxiety and lower self-esteem than those who weren't. In fact, active disrespect was shown, to a statistically significant degree, to have more and clearer consequences for well-being than mere deficits of consideration from bosses.

(For readers interested in the numbers, I present a selected few of the correlations: reported disrespect and depression, .64; reported disrespect and anxiety, .58; reported disrespect and self-esteem, −.45. A comment for those unfamiliar with the study of statistics is that these correlations are quite high—bosses' disrespect accounted for approximately 20 to 40 percent of the variance in individuals' measures of depression, anxiety, and self-esteem—and, again, statistically stronger than those obtained using tests for considerate boss behavior.)[5]

Numbers can establish an argument's scientific credibility, but stories paint a real-life picture. Vanessa, for example, was treated disrespectfully by her boss and suffered personally as a result.

These days it's called sexual harassment; in 1980, my boss called it being my mentor. He was the president of the organization, and I reported to him as a director. Over the course of a year his notes, flowers, phone calls, and presents increased, always wrapped in the guise of his being a supportive manager. He could never own up to what he was doing. Everything came to a head when he appeared on my doorstep one night. He'd come back early from a business trip and instead of going home to his wife, he came to my house, expecting to spend the night. I refused, although I was afraid of making my refusal too explicit and losing my job.

Afterward I became very depressed. I was exhausted—gradually able to work only about five hours a day, while I slept about twelve hours a day, lost ten pounds, and developed skin rashes and a cloudiness, like a film, over my right eye. After several eye exams, which revealed nothing, I finally found a doctor who told me what happens with prolonged depression. I got back into therapy and within a month or so was getting some relief from my symptoms.

The symptoms experienced by Vanessa, other women who have been sexually harassed, and thousands of victims of other instances of boss abuse are all strikingly similar. In addition to the effects on anxiety, depression, and self-esteem, abused subordinates commonly report gastrointestinal disorders, headaches, dermatological reactions, lack of sleep, and sexual dysfunction.

A pertinent bit of evidence that hones these findings concerns the extent to which tough, stern bosses who are *not* actively disrespectful affect their subordinates' reported levels of depression, anxiety, and self-esteem. *They don't.* The correlation is essentially zero. Evidently, having a boss who is demanding but not mean-spirited or disrespectful has no bearing whatsoever on individual well-being.

Skeptics might be wondering whether testimonies of bosses' abuse could be simply in the eye of the beholder. The argument would be that regardless of bosses' actual behaviors, depressed and anxious subordinates with comparatively low levels of self-esteem will tend to see their bosses as abusive because of their own psychological states, not based on actual mistreatment by their bosses. An interesting possibility, but it's not so, according to a research team who explored the possibility. Professor John Michela's team's investigation led to two main conclusions that fundamentally contradict the "beholder's eye" theory. First, they found that subordinates of the same boss tend to see him or her similarly, regardless of the employees' preexisting psychological states. Their second finding was that workers with the same boss exhibit similar empirical levels of depression, anxiety, and self-esteem. It is reasonable to conclude, therefore, that the toxin afflicting subordinates' well-being originates in bosses' misbehavior and not in any emotionally skewed misperception by the victims.

WORK CONSEQUENCES

A common and disturbing outcome of disrespectful abuse at work is that the wound it inflicts on workers' confidence and sense of self can disable them, interfering significantly with their on-the-job performance.

I was working as a training director, and reported to the vice-president of human resources, Dudley. Even though my credibility was very high, a consultant friend of Dudley's decided that the competency of the trainers was in question, so he arranged a training program which would certify everyone. I had been working with these people formally and informally for the previous four years on their training skills. When it came time to certify, he told me that I had to participate like everyone else. People were concerned, saying, "Marsha, I don't understand. Why aren't you helping him? What's going on?"

I had to do a presentation like the rest, and it was unusually good, based on feedback from the group. Dudley sat in a corner of the room while each trainer met individually with the consultant, who told me that my work wasn't good enough. I asked why, and the best answer he could give was "Well, look at this." He thrust the paper in my face with disgust. "You chose the word pick *instead of choose." The remark was so ridiculous, Dudley actually broke out laughing and tried to muffle it by covering his mouth. I was stunned. How could this man, my boss of four years, sit there and not defend my work? Some of the trainers who had only been training for two months were certified. I was not. Dudley had hired the consultant to get rid of me. It was obvious.*

I was a nervous wreck from then on, frightened of losing my job altogether. I felt a loss of self-esteem, a feeling of not being valued, an almost paranoid fear of being physically harmed. Had I really done a horrible job? Was I the cause of all those problems? Was it my total lack of skill that had created this mess?

First, let's stick to a simple idea: Self-esteem involves self-evaluation, and it represents an individual's beliefs about three things—his or her potency (or *efficacy*), ability, and worth. Second, let's eliminate a common myth: Even in the presumably "materialistic" society of the United States, research evidence shows that pay is not necessarily associated with individual self-esteem, and neither is the prestige of one's occupation. Rather, employees' self-esteem is tied to social and psychological conditions of work, particularly their experience of supportive relationships, beliefs about others' evaluations of them, and the freedom to exercise independent judgment.[6]

For subordinates, of course, bosses are in a unique position to exert influence in each of these realms. If they elect to treat their employees with abusive disrespect, then their bludgeoning detracts from workers' sense of potency; their belittling harms workers' sense of ability; and their betrayals undermine workers' feeling of worth.

The consequence is that employees with lowered self-esteem become organizational liabilities.

Self-esteem is not factored into organizations' profit-and-loss statements, but the cost is real nonetheless. Bosses who degrade their subordinates rob both the workers and their organizations of valuable assets. Research findings demonstrate that employees with lower self-esteem exhibit less vigor in their dealings with adversity and generate fewer productive responses in pursuit of challenging goals. They are also more vulnerable to pressures of social conformity and, as a result, are less forthcoming as contributors and problem solvers.

Workers who have been brutally humbled are not the ideal teammates to have when you are crouching in some organizational bunker fighting for your vocational life. They perform less well under stress, have poorer interpersonal skills and initiative, and are less friendly and ambitious. Along with this panoply of hazards to work performance comes at least one specific and grave health tariff: Employees robbed of their self-esteem are more frequently afflicted with heart disease.[7]

Disrespectful abuse by bosses is clearly more than a breach of good manners. It is an assault on individual well-being and organizational productivity. Intimidation, one of the key components of abuse, erodes subordinates' faith in themselves. Intimidated workers relinquish autonomy and work hard to avoid being hit by their boss's other shoe when it drops, forgoing self-direction in favor of self-protection. Instead of exercising self-control, they yield, gripped by passivity and restraint, to a boss's control. Subordinates who are bludgeoned, belittled, and betrayed—as well as dehumanized, blamed, and pummeled with rationalized mistreatment—learn quickly to survive

by advancing with extreme caution, reducing their exposure to bosses' wrath by employing as little independent
judgment and discretion as possible.

One of the intriguing possibilities uncovered by investigations of abusive bosses is that the personal and organizational harm that these bosses cause seems to afflict
even subordinates who are *not* their direct targets. Joel,
senior executive of a *Fortune* fifty company, was working
in one of his company's overseas facilities when his boss,
a man known for "his cruelty, bloodbaths, and belittling
of everyone," visited from the stateside corporate head-
quarters. Dinner arrangements were made and misunder-
stood. Joel, with drinks and hors d'oeuvres attractively
assembled, waited at home for his boss's arrival while
his boss waited for Joel in the lobby of his hotel. When
the snafu at last became clear, Joel rushed to his car and
urged his driver to speed to his boss's hotel.

*When we arrived, he was waiting outside the hotel and
was livid with rage. There was no forgiveness. He humiliated me over and over again throughout the evening, in
front of my driver, going to and from the dinner, in front
of others at the dinner. He never stopped talking about it.
He used insults and called me all sorts of names. "How
stupid can you be?" "What kind of idiot are you?" "Idi-
ots like you can't manage a dinner arrangement, how can
you manage this operation?"*

*My stomach was in knots. It was degrading and un-
called-for. I thought about it for a long time. It was a real
blow to my dignity as a person.*

*Now, my driver had been with the company for twenty-
six years. He was a tough man, a wartime hero, and what
happened to him was amazing and totally unpredictable.*

He disappeared from work, and no one knew where he was or what happened. Believe me, it was incredible, but two years later he showed up in my office, crying, still humiliated and shamed because of what he saw happen to me. He'd completely collapsed because of it.

WORK IS MURDER

Bosses' abuse causes terrible consequences for its victims—and even, it seems, for its witnesses. Farfetched as it may seem, one such outcome may be worksite homicide.

Given that the U.S. Bureau of Labor Statistics ranks it as second in causes of workplace deaths in the United States, and that in 1993, for instance, 1,063 people were murdered at work,[8] it may come as a surprise that there is a debate over whether workplace homicide is in fact a crisis.[9] But as for our concern, whether bosses' brutality should be implicated in workplace homicide, events at the U.S. Post Office provide relevant evidence.

Between 1983 and 1993, ten postal employees went on homicidal rampages, murdering thirty-four supervisors and co-workers.[10] Certainly, a postal employee's job is not without its technical challenges, physical effort, and pressured pace. But can anyone claim that these work demands are that much worse than those encountered in the myriad of job settings where no homicidal rampages have occurred? A natural conclusion is that it is the way in which post office work is managed, and not the content of the work itself, that caused these horrific human explosions.[11]

Employees interviewed at an Oklahoma post office, for

instance, reported problems with their bosses, characterizing them as unfair, infantilizing, autocratic, and even physically abusive. They said that electronic surveillance systems monitored and controlled behavior in ways that crossed the lines of reason and respect. No one could move from a work station without punching in and punching out. There was no trust. Words like *military* were used in order to describe the kinds of controls being employed by bosses, and firings and suspensions were common forms of punishment. One worker identified his mistreatment by bosses as the cause of sleep and eating disruptions that eventually required him to seek psychotherapy. Many believed that their bosses' behaviors ultimately contributed to their co-workers' homicidal rampages.

The irony of the scenario is tragic. The abused, treated as if they were not entitled to the ordinary rights of community members, finally act barbarously and confirm their status as outsiders to the civilized community.

Subordinate reactions to abusive boss behavior, from headaches to homicide, reveal an enduring aspect of people's work experience: Healthy social relations are vital. Mistreatment by bosses will provoke a response, internal if not external, self-destructive rather than constructive. And the arsenal of bosses who inflict this mistreatment is expanding.

CHAPTER FIVE

HIGH-TECH
ABUSE:
Coping with Electronic Assault

The siege mentality of bosses has been worsened by their personal experiences in today's turbulent business environment. Now more than ever, their inclination is to sneak about in organizational bunkers and keep ever-closer watch over subordinate behavior. Lately this defensive obsession has resulted in E-mail assaults and electronic monitoring.

The growing availability of electronic communications has in many cases fueled the flames of abusive boss behavior. Some might have expected it to aid in squelching this fire, reasoning that opportunity for rapid contact and direct response diminishes any stress caused by lack of information. But technological progress has never produced Nirvana. E-mail, for example, one of the most prominent innovations at American workplaces, has brought with it a phenomenon known, appropriately, as "flaming."[1]

FLAMING

Flaming is based on impulsive anger, a malady that is likely to infect bosses who suffer stress. E-mail messages that constitute flaming are rapid, rabid, and, when they come from bosses, harmful to subordinates' well-being. Several respondents mentioned abusive EMs (electronic mail messages) from bosses. One EM that was handed to me by Donna came from a boss described as being at her wits' end.

Her plate was full. Her own boss was on her back for overdue work: She was under so much pressure that she'd become forgetful and disorganized. What she asked us to do in turn was incomplete and confusing. I had sent her an EM with a list of seven questions that I had about the timing and sequencing of deliverables, staffing, implications of certain work for other units. Anyway, I kept the response that I got. I know it was prepared pretty much as soon as she received my EM.

She accused me of being "indecisive" and unable to "assume delegated responsibility." To prove it, she took each question and answered them with things like: "Better attention at meetings" or "If someone paid attention to details, they would know this." She called the questions "stupid" and "the product of incompetence, malingering, or both." The thing was the tone. I don't think I'd

*overlooked any information, since a lot was actually un-
available to me and she had been unclear, but she was so
irate and insulting. I felt like nothing. For a while I
couldn't get it out of my head. It was totally distracting.*

Often the story ends here. This one, however, continues on to a happy ending: A few days later, Donna's boss
apologized—also, fittingly, by EM.

GOTCHA: DISCIPLINE VERSUS DEVELOPMENT

Electronic surveillance of worksite activity is a rapidly
growing enterprise. In the United States alone, current
gross revenues have soared beyond a half billion dollars.
Such monitoring affects the work lives of more than ten
million employees in more than 70,000 companies. Although a large proportion of these ten million are currently clerical workers, the practice is rapidly spreading
to include surveillance of professional, technical, and
managerial employees.[2]
Can anyone justify all this effort and expense? Advocates think so, claiming that monitoring provides an
accurate means of making objective assessments of performance. By recording product counts, errors made, and
time per task, supervisors can then track worker ability,
provide feedback, and increase productivity. Opponents
of electronic surveillance point to evidence that shows
that close monitoring is associated with increases in
stress and dissatisfaction, as well as decreases in morale,
teamwork, and—a direct contradiction to the claims of
advocates—*productivity.* Appealing as well to ethics and

law, opponents argue that monitoring breaches workers' rights to privacy. Both sides refer to discrepancies in research findings to prove their points,[3] but the most important element in this debate is the presence or absence of *Gotcha* goals. It is this organizational agenda—the *why* and not the *what* of electronic monitoring systems—that determines how bosses introduce and use them and how they will affect workers.

Electronic monitoring systems represent *Gotcha* goals when their purpose is to provide justification for disciplining employees and to create a "paper trail" used to legitimate punishment. Evidence of the effect of *Gotcha* goals is contained in a statement from a manager who worked at one of the Baby Bells, a regional telephone company that was born with the breakup of AT&T.

We did it all wrong, like vinegar on waffles. The plan was simple enough: monitoring work without anybody knowing that we were using electronic paraphernalia of all sorts—kind of an old-style time and motion study, really—would provide some accurate account of productivity. Lordy, what a shock! It knocked us off one wall and into another.

First, no one was to know. But it turns out that everyone knew, probably even before the ON *button was pushed. Of course, what they believed was only part right, but that didn't matter. They were right enough about the equipment and what it all could do. Believe me, individual records and the like were absolutely not in the cards. Joan and James could be lazing about, or running around like scared hares, and we never would have known, nor did we actually care to. Information about individuals was irrelevant and of absolutely no value to our purpose. But workers had it in their heads that our purpose was to keep track of individuals, and no amount of persuasion was going to change that. I cannot begin to tell you about the agitation that was caused, or the creativity which went into beating the system. You got to love folks for that kind of ingenuity. We had one heck of a protest.*

It came from the hurt. That's what made them so sad and angry: feeling that they were being shut out and spied upon, with no say-so whatsoever, because they couldn't be trusted.

Why were the Baby Bell employees so upset? The reality is that, formally or informally, electronically or not, bosses have always monitored subordinates' work activity. So what's the big deal? Why are these increasingly popular, high-tech forms of electronic surveillance any different from the overseeing of work in the past? The difference is that they give Big Brother Boss the capacity to watch all of the workers all of the time, without any of them knowing that it's happening. In these days of downsizing, cost control, and crowded markets, that capacity becomes an irresistible crutch for bosses lacking the leadership skills, personal energy, or organizational resources that are needed to motivate subordinates. It provides bosses with what appears to be an objective and foolproof means of secretly recording and thus controlling behavior. Make a wrong move and they've *gotcha*.

Gotcha goals are damaging not only because they intimidate and threaten subordinates with punishment, but also because they contain implicitly demeaning commentary about the subordinates as people. The message is: "Workers cannot be expected to perform ably and honestly without the use of monitoring as a whip." Surveillance geared toward *Gotcha* goals resurrects an image of subordinates as an untrustworthy, lazy, stupid lot who prefer play over work. And as the late Douglas McGregor established in his book *The Human Side of Enterprise,*[4] bosses who treat their subordinates with such coercion and obsessive control often produce among workers the very behaviors that they were hoping to avoid. Harry Levinson, another analyst of behavior in organizations, arrived at the same conclusion in his book *The Great Jackass Fallacy*[5]: that bosses who use carrot-and-stick motivational strategies may actually foster, instead of the intended obedience, a "jackass" attitude of anger and resistance among them.

The alternative to *Gotcha* goals is the use of information gleaned electronically as a tool for *developing* performance rather than disciplining performers. This alternative requires credible limits to be placed on organizations' use of surveillance technology. Nations like Norway and Sweden have already done so; but in the United States, we have just begun to establish such regulations in the face of considerable opposition. The "Privacy for consumers and workers act," HR1218, must do battle with the attitudes of lawmakers like former Secretary of Labor Lynn Martin, who argued for the maintenance of a hands-off policy toward bosses. "We strongly believe," she said, "that in our economic system, employers must continue to have great latitude in deciding the best means of evaluating their employees and their service to the public, maintaining business productivity, ensuring workplace security, and otherwise managing their enterprises."[6]

It is poor counsel, in this case, to encourage the full exercise of bosses' legal latitude. Limits on electronic monitoring should be guided by what is productive, not permissible. Lawyers and legislatures may debate and ultimately resolve the legal intricacies of electronic surveillance. But for right now, high- and low-tech abuse that result in assaults on individuals must be addressed by people committed to organizational success. These assaults are a cause of workers' deteriorating mental and physical health and work performance, and require immediate remedy.

About ten years ago, when E-mail was probably still only a gleam in someone's eye, my first boss put together this great little team—cooperative, supportive, even when we disagreed with one another. I was pretty anxious to do well, being a new engineer, working in an industry that I really didn't know very well. My boss and co-workers couldn't have been more helpful.

After about six or seven weeks the boss moved. It was a terrific promotion for him, but one that put him under real pressure. His replacement was a controlling, one-on-one type. Always with him there was a sense of "So, what did you do for me today?" Anyway, my old boss and I met by accident one day and talked about how the change was affecting him. He spoke of his woes—the stress was visible. After, I sent him a note: "Nice seeing you, hang in there," that kind of thing. You know, friendly, supportive.

Now my new boss calls me into his office and chews me out for using interoffice mail for personal purposes. I'm bewildered. What is he referring to? *I wonder. Finally he alludes to my former boss and a light goes on in my head. I asked, "Do you mean that note?" He nodded. He was reading our mail.*

Others had similar experiences. He just devastated our group. We had no way of knowing to what extent it was happening. I was so furious that it made me feel light-headed, disoriented, nauseous. I felt raped. There was no way that the S.O.B. would get more work from me than I needed to do just to stay out of harm's way or get a new job.

E-mail is no longer a gleam in anyone's eye, nor is the world of surveillance software, a large part of the electronic surveillance industry with more than $175 million in reported revenues in the United States and a projected five-year growth of 50 percent per year.[7] With surveillance software, bosses anywhere can view subordinates' E-mail and other work at any time without the workers' knowledge or approval. If ruthless access to personal correspondence is a kind of "rape," then high-tech developments permit mass-rape with increasing efficiency.

The monitoring of mail, E-mail, conversations, and telephone calls may in fact produce results. Subordinates' discontent and disapproval of their companies and bosses may be detected; personal use of company resources, in violation of policy, may be documented; and, occasionally, criminal breaches of security may be uncovered. Yet the "great latitude" of those in charge must have its limits. The fruits of covert electronic monitoring are few and far between, for the most part, and are accompanied by far more likely health and productivity costs. Furthermore, any discontent, disapproval, or dysfunctional behavior discovered under surveillance is often the symptom of underlying organizational problems that merit remedial attention, and that are not cured by punishing workers.

During the 1930s, long before computers and E-mail and electronic surveillance were common in the workplace, a boundary was crossed by organizational monitoring, and a woman I know suffered. With a few years of work experience, prodigious skills as a statistical typist, and financial pressures stemming from the nation's economic depression, my mother-in-law, then in her twenties, found a job at a "communications giant" only by masquerading as a non-Jew. She quickly emerged as a successful and popular employee, but her vocational success was short-lived. Coming from a religiously observant family, she could not work on Rosh Hashanah and Yom Kippur; so, continuing the deception, she followed company procedure and called in sick on those days.

One holiday, the doorbell at her home rang, and when she heard that the surprise visitor was a supervisor from the office, she ran to change out of her clothing for services while her mother politely offered coffee and cakes. When the modest snack arrived, along with my mother-in-law, the visitor said with a glance toward her employee, "What nice little *Jewish* cakes these are." My mother-in-law lost her job soon afterward.

This tale is not ancient history. Her attempt to avoid persecution—in this case religious—and her company's brazen entrance into her home and personal life are mirrored today, over and over, in higher-tech but no more subtle invasions of workers' privacy. Documented examples from the 1990s abound. Northern Telecom, according to claims made by the Communication Workers of America, spied on its employees by listening in on telephone calls made on both business and public phones on the premises.[8] In Illinois, forty-three Kmart workers sued the company when it hired a detective agency to track the activities of employees. While Kmart claims it did so to combat theft, the employees and their attorney disagree, contending that reports submitted by the detective agency included information on employee attitudes regarding unions and on shopping habits, recreational activities, and living arrangements. Some evidence, it was claimed, was collected by spies disguised as employees. "You feel betrayed by the company," said Lewis Hubbell, a Kmart employee for twenty-eight years. "You expect this in communist countries. But you don't expect it from Kmart."[9] While organizations publicly claim that the sole purpose of electronic eavesdropping is to prevent stealing and to watch over customer service, the potential for more abusive uses is enormous.

Organizations may need the kind of information that electronic monitoring can provide. But the net value of that information to both employers and employees is not only comprised of the content and accuracy of *what* is discovered but also of *how* the information is acquired. The lesson to be learned from organizations that have made effective use of electronic monitoring is that *Gotcha* goals must be abandoned, and development, not discipline, must be the purpose of surveillance.

EFFECTIVE ELECTRONIC MONITORING: A GUIDE

Following four operational guidelines prevents the dominance of *Gotcha* goals, promotes employee improvement, and permits organizations to use electronic monitoring to their advantage.

1. *Put subordinates' finger on the buttons.* In 1993, an experiment reported in the *Journal of Applied Social Psychology* investigated how the task performance of seventy-two women, all university students, was affected by electronic monitoring. The productivity of women who were monitored was markedly inferior to that of the other women in the control group who worked free of surveillance. However, when the women who were monitored in this experiment were given *control* over when they would be monitored, and when the surveillance was applied to the whole group and not only to individuals within the group, their task performance improved 40 percent.[10] When we consider how much less are the pressure, the motivations, and the vulnerability of university students taking part in a lab experiment than those of real employees on the job, these findings are powerful testimony to how negative the effects of monitoring can be when it's for real.

   The lesson provided by the experiment, and by experience with electronic monitoring at a number of worksites, is a confirmation of the need for more subordinate control of worker surveillance. In fact, performance has been proven to benefit even when the control given to subordinates is indirect, in the form of information about when monitoring will occur. At one of the Baby Bells, for example, procedures were introduced that simply let operators know when monitoring would happen and also allowed them to choose between remote monitoring and personal monitoring by a supervisor. The effect of introducing these indirect forms of control was a reported rise in the quality of performance both when the monitoring light was on and when it was off.[11]

Why did the operators' performance improve rather than slacken—the inverse of the reaction to covert monitoring? When bosses hand subordinates the button, they are also passing along an implicit message that contradicts the view of workers as "jackasses." Instead, it shows workers their bosses' positive evaluation of their commitment, reliability, and trustworthiness. This boost of confidence, combined with greater autonomy and the freedom to adjust the pace and activities of one's own labor, makes for a more productive worker.

2. *Monitor the group rather than the individual.* Electronic monitoring systems that single out individuals for observation are more likely to be in pursuit of *Gotcha* goals than those that collect information about group performance.

Avis's telephone representatives process thousands of inquiries about car rental fees, special discounts, and vehicle availability. For the business to run smoothly, the information they give to callers must be delivered swiftly and accurately. In order to improve their service, Avis's phone conversations are monitored; but whole offices, not individual representatives, are the target of data collection and analysis.[12] The result appears to be useful information for improving performance without the adverse psychological effects on employees.

Professor Jack Aiello, a leading authority on the use

of electronic monitoring systems in organizations, reports that in Japan, although there are not prohibitions restricting the use of these systems, the strong preference among companies is to monitor groups rather than single workers. In 1987, a report from the Office of Technological Assessment of the United States Congress identified a similar trend in this country. The report, titled "The Electronic Supervisor: New Technology, New Tension," pointed out that union pressure has produced a shift from the monitoring of individuals to that of collective work performance. Such a trend is heartening, but we should not be fooled; a broadening of the scope of surveillance alone will not do the job. Bucking *Gotcha* goals requires organizations to pay sincere attention to all four of these guidelines.

3. *Have co-workers, not bosses, make use of the information.* Avis is a company that is not widely suspected of *Gotcha* goals. This is partly because of its group monitoring, as described, and also because the surveillance and coaching of new agents is done by co-workers with a history of experience in that job. A similar technique is reported to be used at an AT&T site in the eastern United States.[13] Here, approximately one thousand telephone operators are cooperating in a project in which more experienced workers monitor and advise less experienced ones. This surveillance is met with enthusiasm, not wariness, as it is instituted to promote productivity rather than to enforce hierarchy.

   Suspicion of *Gotcha* goals is decreased when the principal users of electronically monitored data are co-workers, and when their sole purpose is to upgrade work skills. An emphasis on employee development makes electronic monitoring procedures like the ones used at Avis and AT&T vastly different from other approaches that stress discipline and reestablish subordinate inferiority and subjugation, turning bosses into sneaky overlords with electronic whips.

4. *Development, development, development.* When subordinates believe that their own development is truly the objective of electronic surveillance, the level of secrecy surrounding monitoring seems to be less critical. Reports from Toyota Motor Sales maintain that customer service representatives are subject to silent monitoring a couple of times each month. Immediately after the monitoring, however, there is a data feedback session in which workers' strengths and areas in need of improvement are identified. At Charles Schwab, too, conversations between brokers and clients are commonly recorded. From time to time, with no warning, agents listen to the live conversations. While the recordings provide a necessary record of transactions, the periodic listening-in by agents serves as the basis for ensuing discussions on how to improve the quality of customer service. At the General Electric Answer Center in Louisville, Kentucky—said in 1991 to be receiving 14,000 telephone calls daily from people needing information on GE products—the phone responses of more than two hundred employees were silently monitored on occasion. The clear purpose of the monitoring was to provide information for a review of the way calls were handled and what could be modified.

A whopping 96 percent customer satisfaction rating argues that the folks at GE were doing something right.

The center's manager reported that each call costs the company $4 but yields $16 in sales and savings from service calls that don't have to be made.[14] That's not a bad ratio, one which would likely be out of reach if the Answer Center had embraced *Gotcha* goals instead of developmental ones.

Even when they are earnest in their pursuit of developmental goals, organizations must take care to monitor the work activity that needs development and not only that which is most easily measured. Typing speed and customer turnover, two examples of easily (and often) monitored work functions, may have little to do with quality of service. In fact, gains in capacities like these two may actually harm organizational success because they may be associated with declines in accuracy and in individual attention paid to customers. GE's Answer Center in Louisville reports that 70 percent of the criteria used in evaluating phone representatives have to do with the quality of the conversation that they have with callers, and only 15 percent have to do with the number of calls concluded.[15] If these percentages were reversed, it's a safe bet that the exchanges would be more curt and rude, representatives would be more hurried and harried, and the ratio of cost to gain would not be one to four.

Clearly, the acceptance and effectiveness of monitoring systems in organizations depends as much, and perhaps more, on social psychology than on electronic technology. Subordinates' positive or negative responses to surveillance are primarily determined by the purpose to which the technology is put, not by the efficiency of chips and consoles. A decision by bosses to use the technology in the pursuit of discipline and

Gotcha goals is likely to have adverse effects on workers and their performance. When, instead, bosses apply the four guidelines of effective surveillance, it may well become a tool that benefits subordinate well-being, development, and ultimate productivity.

CHAPTER SIX

PROTECTING ABUSERS AND PUNISHING THE ABUSED

"**W**hy do you think of it as abuse?" The well-dressed, sixty-three-year-old retiree was showing signs of annoyance with me. "Someone has got to do the dirty work." Speaking of a former colleague of his, he asserted, "I don't necessarily approve of how he treated people, but, if he was abusive, then so were we all. Because the only difference between him and the rest of us was that he did what we were wishing would happen."

Organizations of all kinds keep a comfortable place for bosses who will do their "dirty work." Nearly half of the employees I spoke with told of organizational condonement of bosses who brutally oppressed subordinates. These dirty-work specialists are the ones whom others rely on to fix a situation without sentimentality, by bulldozing, screaming, and knocking heads if necessary. They were characterized by one interviewee as "SOBs who have a single aim, to build their reputations, while passing the costs onto co-workers and the organization."

Not all the costs, however, are passed along. Bosses who are dirty-work specialists (or SOBs, if you prefer) are likely to earn others' disapproval—sometimes muted, and almost always hypocritical—expressed in the familiar nickname "hatchet men/women." These bosses act on behalf of a constituency who are themselves then mercifully freed from doing the organization's dirty work and enabled to disapprove self-righteously of such brutality. Meanwhile, the bosses with clean hands feel fully justified in not acting to prevent the ax from crashing, because "someone has to do the dirty work." For these bosses, the arrangement could not be better. By keeping someone around to perform the unsightly and brutal tasks, they get their cake, eat it, and are able to avoid confronting their own guilt in the degradation of co-workers and subordinates. The process, functioning like a perverse organizational immune system, is fed by bosses' self-interest. They close ranks against the workers below them, driven by three distinct cravings: profit, power, and self-protection.

PROFIT

Songs and proverbs remind us of the relationship between clouds and silver linings. Regrettably, there are times when the clouds of abusive boss behavior line the pockets of organizational bystanders with enough silver to buy their support and their teamwork against subordinate foes.

Just recently, I witnessed a bunch of people, including me—and I'm ashamed of that—not just close their eyes to abuse, but actually support it through their inaction. We were ratifying a decision to appoint a regional executive. You may have seen the appointment announced—in the Journal, *I think. What that story didn't say, and what the media had no way of knowing, is that despite his business success, our appointee is like a serial killer. He has pushed more people overboard than anyone I know or have ever heard of. He is ruthless and, when it comes to other human beings, insensitive and heartless.*

In our discussion, the issue of his character was brought up in an almost embarrassed way. Then the inevitable b.s.: "He does the job"; "It's only two or three years till retirement"; "What's important here, his manner or his performance?" Why create a fuss with someone you've rewarded all along? You see, companies become dependent on such people—you don't want to admit it, but you do. I'm sure people spoke to him about his people-management skills during his career, but really nothing was done about it. I personally know four or five very successful people who left the company after being chewed up and spit out by this person.

The fact is that bosses like him get a slap on the wrist at most. His treatment of people should not have been condoned for twenty years, much less rewarded.

Linda Wachner, Warnaco CEO, also has a reputation for being able to chew people up. "I've yelled at people," she proclaimed, "and I'm not ashamed of it. We have to run this company efficiently and without a bunch of babies who say, 'Mommy yelled at me today.' It's impossible to run a leveraged operation like a camp. If you don't like it, leave."[1] Evidently, to Ms. Wachner, profit is prime, dulling whatever pain a boss's misbehavior might cause for subordinates. When *Fortune* magazine wanted to feature Ms. Wachner's management style in an article about harsh bosses, she had her CFO and her controller tell the writers that they had become rich because of her. It is a view shared by many bosses: A profitable end justifies any managerial means. Humiliated and abused subordinates have no reason to gripe as long as they're paid.

An interview with a thirty-seven-year-old manager in a consumer products company illustrated another rationalization of abusive bosses who look out solely for each other. He told me of a conversation with an associate concerning Sam, a supervisor.

I entered a conference room. Sam's whole group was standing stiffly around the table at attention and Sam was seated, firing questions at them, cutting off answers, using words like "dunce" and "dimwit." He had a reputation for this sort of thing, but this was the only time that I saw it firsthand. Afterward, when the opportunity arose, I told my associate what had happened, intending to leave the matter in her hands. But how she responded was incredible to me.

"He's not to blame," she said. "Do you think that he likes coming down so hard on these people? But it's necessary, not just for the organization, which depends on them doing the right thing, but for them. They're safer knowing that they can't get away with anything."

I must have looked at her like she was crazy. But she wasn't. She was just one of many someones who wanted to get the job done—meet the bottom line and damn all else. As if Sam's way were the only way to do it. She didn't care the slightest bit about anyone—not Sam's workers, not me, not really the organization.

"He probably loses sleep," she went on. "His people are really to blame. You've got to whip it to them, otherwise they don't learn or produce."

The story is testimony to the reservoir of reasons available to people who want to justify and cover up their complicity in the abuse of other human beings. Onlookers whose gains cause them to stand mute as employees suffer at the hands of those doing the dirty work find comfort and preservation of their self-image in business-related reasons for the abuse. "It's not my way," they say. "Of course I don't approve, and I wouldn't do it myself, but someone has to kick tail once in a while. Workers need to be brought in line, straightened out, whipped into shape." Occasionally they will offer the hollow prediction that, with more experience, the abusive boss will *mature* and *mellow*. Considering organizations' greed-driven, positive reinforcement of mistreatment by bosses, it is a promise that is unlikely to be fulfilled.

POWER

Concerns about their own power push some bosses to become hypersensitive to anything that smells, feels, looks, sounds, or tastes like insubordination. When they imagine some revolt to be directed at them, they are fast to take measures that will nip it in the bud, working with other bosses to end the "uprising" before it grows into a danger for them all. It often comes down to a power struggle between an *in* group (of bosses) and an *out* group (of subordinates), with the bosses vehemently protecting their own—even when their own are obviously guilty of flagrant abuse and the perceived insubordination is really no more than workers' efforts to defend themselves.

I worked for a boss who used my performance evaluation as a way to punish me for what she said was a lack of loyalty. When I received the evaluation, I asked her why, in the face of glowing reviews by internal customers, she would give me such a poor evaluation. She said, "Because you're not loyal." She was very uncertain about her status and respect from others. By raising questions about major conceptual issues in the work process, I was being disloyal, she thought. There may also have been some racism here, as she had not been exposed to highly educated minority people.

After that I was constantly watched for mistakes so that she could build a paper trail to replace me. I felt harassed. There was no politeness or civility, only tension. But I was skeptical about an appeal. My experience is that there is rarely such a thing as a successful appeal. Senior people don't like to admit that any of them have been wrong. No matter what happens, you're the problem—to complain makes you a problem person and your career can suffer even more. I've seen it happen.

Workers' approach to bosses' paranoia of mutiny is further complicated by top-down redefinitions of what qualifies as insubordination. A senior executive in a *Fortune* top-ten company made the point when he characterized his superiors as "children."

"I want things done for me," they say. They are practically helpless. They expect nurturing. If you don't do minor things, it is defiance, and they don't like it. Minor things turn out to be important, personal needs—picking up luggage, for example. It's humiliating, but if you hesitate, much less object, it's a personal insult to them and a challenge to their authority. They feel disrespected and they feel free to abuse you because of it.

Bosses' efforts to team up to keep their powers safe from imagined threat is often accomplished at great cost. The expense of such stonewalling often includes not only blows to employees' self-esteem but drops in company efficiency and even perversions of common sense. Professor Jerry Harvey, famed for his instructive story *The Abilene Paradox,* writes of an organization in which, after the announcement of a management decision to downsize, 80 percent of the employees voted to take a 20 percent pay cut in order to avoid the firings. The CEO, supported by the managers, rejected the offer. Why? Reportedly because changing a decision on the basis of "sentimental human considerations" like keeping people employed would compromise the free exercise of management prerogative in the future.[2] Preoccupations with power are not as rational as they are common among bosses who insulate themselves and each other against the workers beneath them.

SELF-PROTECTION

People in powerful posts often secure their positions by joining together to displace blame for mistakes onto those with less power. Recent behavior by CEO Robert Crandall and other senior executives at American Airlines seems to be an example of that trick.[3] Some say that these bosses blamed flight attendants for an annual loss of approximately $1.2 billion. More likely, the falloff was caused by this executive group's decision the previous year to expand both the airline's fleet and its terminals while cutting fares by 50 percent. Such apparent scapegoating is offensive, but, in the light of other supporting data, not surprising. For instance, in 1992 Professor Warren Boeker used data from sixty-seven organizations, gathered during a twenty-two-year period, to show that when performance in these organizations deteriorated, less powerful executives were far more likely to be dismissed than powerful ones.[4] Evidently, the more powerful bosses survived by blaming their companies' declining fortunes on subordinates, many of whom lost their jobs in the process.

Bosses may also protect themselves by defending abusive peers in whom they have made an investment. They ignore complaints and even disregard reason to let someone else take the fall instead of one of their own.

My boss had been hand-picked by senior people in our section to head the project. Others regarded him as a very political person: very, very oriented to satisfying superiors no matter what. When I was appointed to the job, my boss and I discussed the project's objectives and the contribution that our function could make. He wanted to play a political game, not wanting to commit ourselves in case things worked out badly. Not really supporting the effort. I wanted to engage in earnest, providing our full expertise and a real commitment—it was important for the organization. I went ahead on that basis, trying at the same time to protect him from any fallout if things didn't work out.

I found out later that he interfered by telling people not to support me, by not passing along my requests, and by bad-mouthing me to superiors. I didn't know it at the time, although it sure felt like I was always walking uphill.

Well, even with all that, the project team's work was a real success by every objective standard. We were all very proud. Team members were very positive about my work. And my boss made sure that he was praised for what I had accomplished.

Now this is why his condemnation of me broke this camel's back. I told him about how disappointed and angry I was. He used the team's success, and my contribution to it, for his gain, but then accused me of things like not developing people skills, not building cross-organizational ties, problems with communication, and being weak on detail. I had received written praise from the project's head on these very criteria. He didn't care about what they said, or how successful I was; what he cared about was that I hadn't done exactly what he had or-dered—even though, at the time, he had said to me, "Do what you think is right." He was giving me an inferior evaluation for disloyalty and for not showing blind obe-dience.

That's when I learned about politics. His hypocrisy was clear, but no one would do anything about him. He's been promoted more than once since this, despite the fact that he has an entirely negative reputation with any-one who is his direct report and even with peers. But he is carried along by this Mafia of bosses who just defend him. They're like, "He's one of the boys. If he's bad, then so are we." So all the feedback and complaints from workers are dismissed by these people. Managers like him are constantly promoted, or protected in sideways moves. While he wasn't perfect, he was the boss. The company had faith in him and were going to back him. He was in fact developing a "good track record." I was a victim, and they said as much, and yet they chose to defend him. Can you believe it?

Yes, I can. It is a common organizational perversion. But the means of discouraging this and other forms of abuse by bosses exist. People and communities can, and must, work toward the eradication of brutality at the workplace.

CHAPTER SEVEN

DISCOURAGING ABUSIVE BOSS BEHAVIOR:

The New Social Compact

1. *What did we do? What's really possible? You work with people in the crew, getting them better at dealing with what was being dished out. But, you know, you can only do so much of that, and you've got to be sensitive: You could actually make it worse for them if the foreman somehow felt threatened.*

2. *There was another thing that we did. We tried to give this foreman some feedback. It was an attempt to discourage what was happening—lots of luck.*

3. *But what else is there? You're talking about loading platforms—a trucking company. Foremen are foremen. Some of them were just that way with their crews. What do we do, change the whole shooting match?*

———

There, in a few words from one interview, is a reasonably complete account of the three prominent approaches to discouraging bosses' abusive behavior. The theme of the first approach is *change the victims.* The *change the victims* approach presumes that since bosses from hell are here to stay, it is their victims who must be responsible for remedial effort. Suggested tactics involve teaching victims how to limit physical exposure to their bosses, and, in the event that evasion fails, advising sufferers on therapeutic, self-help techniques supposed to blunt adverse effects on their mental health and work productivity. The second of the three approaches, involving "feedback," "discouragement," and, I must say, "lots of luck," has a different goal: *change the abusers.* More optimistic than the first approach, this effort presumes that abusive bosses are *not* here to stay, rather that bosses will alter their toxic behavior with proper insight and incentive. And the third attempt to discourage on-the-job abuse—in effect, to "change the whole shooting match" and *change the system*—recognizes that the first two approaches are likely to fail because they focus on changing individuals, victims or abusers.

Forcing people to renovate their attitudes and habits, the *change the system* theory argues convincingly, is impossible without improving the organizational culture that shapes the character of every encounter between bosses and subordinates. Brutal boss behavior is fed and nourished by work arrangements that express a traditional, autocratic, hierarchical culture. Consequently, there will be no meaningful change in either the occurrence or consequence of abuse of subordinates unless the structure of the workplace is reformed according to a new social compact, one that encourages cooperation, justice, and a heightened and broadened sense of community.

To change the whole shooting match is feasible, and it is our best shot at a work environment free of brutality.

CHANGE THE VICTIMS?

Subordinates who are mistreated by their bosses are the recipients of harm, not its agent. Efforts to "educate" subordinate workers about how to cope with their victimization reverse and obscure who is really to blame for the damage being done to their health and productivity.

Constant appeals were made to my boss's superiors for help. I wasn't the first to do it, believe me. Finally, we were called to a meeting without warning, when our boss was away on business or holiday. It must have been planned because they brought in this consultant, a psychologist. These higher-ups probably thought they were helping and responding to our concerns. But we were shocked. She was going to help us think through ways of dealing with difficult bosses, some kind of workshop. But we didn't need help dealing with bosses, it was our boss who needed help. It wasn't our fault and we didn't do anything wrong. To us, it was no abstract exercise: There were wrongs, believe me, but they were being done to us —every day.

I don't care how good my boss was at his job. He needed help, and things needed changing, but I didn't need to sit there with my eyes closed envisioning my "worst and best days"—really. I wasn't busted and I didn't need fixing.

The *change the victims* approach advises abused subordinates to rearrange their exchanges with brutal bosses by either decreasing contact with the boss, increasing contact with others, or getting in contact with oneself.

To decrease head-buttings with bosses, for instance, victimized workers are advised to keep records of the boss's comings and goings, the times of day when she or he is most "difficult," and the particular work issues that act as triggers for the boss's abuse of them. Then, subordinates are urged, allocate your time and activities according to the patterns discovered.[1] Physical contact can be reduced in acceptable (if devious) ways by deliberately scheduling breaks or meetings away from the immediate worksite at bosses' most tense periods. In addition, to avoid triggering a boss's wrath, employees are encouraged to devote disproportionate time to those areas of work that are emotionally explosive for a boss, regardless of subordinates' estimation of work priorities.

There is empirical evidence that burnout at work is worse for employees who lack access to social support systems than for those who have such access.[2] The same effect is likely increased for subordinates who have suffered direct boss abuse. Some advocates of the *change the victims* approach have encouraged abused employees both to seek social support and to give it to co-workers who have been similarly victimized. Based on common sense, this seems reasonable. The humiliation and loss of self-esteem that accompany the silent suffering caused by abusive bosses may be mitigated by seeking contact with colleagues in the same boat. If implicit in a boss's mistreatment is the statement "You are not worthy of the common civility due to community members," then, through their willingness to listen and understand without condemnation, ridicule, or punishment, other people in effect respond, "You are worthy." But, sadly, embarrassment, further oppression, and organizational isolation usually cut off the abused from helpful contact with others.

Another way victims of abuse can make use of relationships with others is to seek a protector among them. Labor union representatives, members of a company's personnel or human resources staff, or an institution's designated ombudspersons are all potential protectors. Successful intervention by such protectors would require clear, verifiable evidence of rule transgression and credible procedures for redress. Even when these elusive conditions exist, wielding protectors may entail significant risk for victims.

A telephone company employee explained the problem succinctly.

You've got to make sure, in your own mind, that it's worth your while, because you can get a reputation as a trouble-maker. If you're getting pushed enough, then of course you take the proper steps. But you can't do that about everything. They can get back at you, you know; there are ways of getting back which won't be complained about by anyone.

Lastly, the suggestion of the *change the victims* approach to get in contact with oneself is based on the hope that victims of boss abuse can dilute the most toxic consequences of their experience through self-insight and relaxation. The instruction is to create an internal dialogue. Instead of suffering humiliation in silence, ask yourself, "Why is my boss's mistreatment of me touching buttons of distress? Why haven't I been able simply to dismiss this person as uncouth and impolite? What am I contributing to the pain that I'm feeling?"

Reflecting more "deeply" on one's treatment by an abusive boss can also entail a worker's examining it in the wider context of her or his life. In order to achieve this shift in perspective, employees may be tutored to focus on other key, satisfying relationships and to explore the relationships' priorities as well as their contrasting messages about social worth.

A few can do it. Even when they are caught up in the flaming hell of boss abuse, some workers can step back and chat with themselves, constructing a mental fire wall between how they feel about themselves and the humiliating victimization they suffer at the hands of their bosses. But most are unable to maintain the extraordinary equilibrium that is necessary for such an internal dialogue.

Even if more subordinates were able to use these ambitious procedures to curtail the adverse effects of toxic encounters with bosses, it is important to ask: Are these schemes to *change the victims* appropriate solutions to the problem of abusive boss behavior? Even when they work to alleviate workers' suffering—and this is rare—they do absolutely nothing to prevent bosses from brutalizing scores of future victims. That is unacceptable.

CHANGE THE ABUSERS?

Some have argued, instead, that an effective remedy to abuse at work must focus on changing the bosses themselves. This, theorists claim, might be accomplished in three ways: one, *talk* to abusive bosses in order to stir within them transforming insight into the cause and consequence of their cruel interpersonal behavior; two, *train* offending bosses to treat their subordinates differently; and three, *grade* bosses' work performance on a scale geared toward the discouragement of abuse and the encouragement of desirable alternatives.

Ruth, a member of the corporate sales group in a cosmetics firm, shed light on the *talking* cure.

What became obvious is that my boss saw me and herself, the only women in the group, as rivals. You know, like I was competing or something. With the men she was considerate. But with me she was short, belligerent, and really, really rude. And cruel. There were nights that I cried. Many.

One day, after our Monday morning meeting, I followed my boss back to her office and spoke with her about what was happening. I told her the truth: that she was on my case. She was humiliating me constantly for doing the same things that others did—while, when they did it, they got corrected but not personally ridiculed. I gave her three or four examples and asked her whether I was doing anything to cause the problem.

But Ruth did not, and—to be safe—could not *confront* her boss.[3] Accusation and retribution were not part of her agenda. Forcibly asserting her rights was not a possibility. She was aware that while giving a boss a talking-to may embolden victims, the risk of igniting an explosive response still exists. The situation is volatile, and subordinates who choose to approach their bosses one-on-one in order to "change" them are clearly playing with fire. The same expertly conducted, nonconfrontational conversations that might work to earn subordinates civil treatment will, at other times, dispose bosses to come down even harder on workers who, they feel, maneuvered them into talks that are out of line.

If abuse of subordinates can be said to occur because bosses lack certain behavioral abilities, then it seems reasonable to design educational *training* sessions to give them the requisite abilities. However, people and organizations choosing to tread this path rely on faith that the desired interpersonal skills are not only identifiable and teachable, but also that they, once learned, will actually be used by bosses on crucial occasions.

Psychologist Dr. Robert Baron, for instance, has formulated guidelines that are being incorporated into training programs designed to counter abuse by bosses through the encouragement of constructive communication.[4] Above all, Dr. Baron advises bosses, "Be specific." Vague generalities are the enemy of constructive communication. Don't label subordinates as "incompetent," "foolish," or "shortsighted"; tell them precisely what they may have done wrong. And don't promise punishment for unchangeable, personal aspects of subordinates—because they're allegedly dumb, lazy, or aged. Implicit questions in bosses' attitudes and reactions, like "Who's to blame?", are examples of deconstructive communication, while a response of "How did it happen?" is more constructive. Baron also recognizes the importance of timing, reminding students that constructive communication works best when it occurs as close to the critical event as possible, when information is still fresh and specifics can be more easily identified.

Baron's and others' *training* cure supposes that bosses will develop requisite skills after they are suitably educated. It also assumes that they will have the necessary personal motivation, self-control, and incentive to employ those skills when appropriate in the future. Occasionally they do, and bosses develop helpful skills and have the personal wherewithal to use them. But far more often, the same factors that undermine the *talking* cure undermine the *training* cure: Intense workplace pressures and/or a boss's malignant desire to harm weaker people short-circuit the attempted reprogramming of abusers.

The common inadequacies of both the *talking* and *training* cures point to the need for organizations to put more power behind their efforts to discourage abuse by bosses. One attempt at such power has been the implementation of performance evaluation systems. The rationale behind this *grading* cure is a crude adaptation of B. F. Skinner's principle of operant conditioning: *Change the reinforcement and changes in behavior will follow.*[5]

Not too long ago, *The Monitor,* a publication of the American Psychological Association, reported that the Ford Motor Company planned to include assessment of "ability to cultivate talent" in its evaluations of managerial performance.[6] Similar appraisals could be made of such criteria as bosses' success in promoting good health, lower levels of stress, or supportive work environments among their workers. Indeed, assessments could be made that would select against the Eight Daily Sins of bosses— Deceit, Constraint, Coercion, Selfishness, Inequity, Cruelty, Disregard, and Deification. If these changes are made in performance criteria, the argument goes, then the emerging appraisal system would possess compelling sanctions against the oppression of subordinates. Bad grades would be a wake-up call to abusive bosses that goes beyond timid talks and toothless training sessions.

If performance appraisal systems had a better record of such success, this argument might be more compelling. But ethical grading systems have not been proven to have any significant effect on brutal behavior,[7] perhaps due to the approach's flawed assumptions. First, faith in performance appraisal systems requires that the evaluator be accurately informed of episodes of bosses' abusive behavior. And unless the misbehavior is observed firsthand, this is unlikely; intimidated, endangered subordinates rarely feel free and empowered to report instances of abuse. Second, the grading system's effectiveness also relies on evaluators' willingness to enforce the judgment and discipline bosses, an equally unsafe bet. As has already been demonstrated, even when subordinates do boldly come forward, a common organizational trick is to protect the abusers and condemn the abused.

One innovation in efforts to provide feedback to bosses, called "upward appraisal," seeks to overcome these failings. Although it comes in various shapes and sizes, upward appraisal's typical components are uncomplicated. Bosses receive a single, detailed set of performance assessments from subordinates, whose responses are aggregated in order to preserve anonymity. Usually working with their own superiors, bosses examine their subordinates' appraisals as they work on developing plans for self-improvement. In this way, upward appraisal at least ensures that abused subordinates have anonymous access to an official channel through which to tell others honestly of their work conditions. However, upward appraisal contains familiar shortcomings, guaranteeing neither bosses' acceptance of the feedback nor their willingness to pursue appropriate corrective action.

"Three hundred sixty-degree feedback," another recent innovation related to the *grading* cure, has the same potentials and problems as upward appraisal. Bosses in organizations using 360-degree feedback (such as Warner-Lambert, Nestlé-Perrier, Pitney Bowes, and parts of AT&T)[8] receive responses from everyone around them —subordinates, peers, bosses, customers, and even family members—through structured questionnaires. Organized simply and often unhinged from pay or promotion decisions, the data are compared by bosses to their own self-ratings. It is a way of telling bosses how they are perceived from various perspectives by a surrounding circle of others, without running the risks inherent in a face-to-face conversation. However, as in the case of upward appraisal, the result of beneficial change is predicated on often unrealistic hopes of bosses' acceptance of and reaction to the feedback. Nonetheless, 360-degree feedback, as well as upward appraisal, deserves to be recognized as a marked improvement on traditional performance appraisal systems—and, furthermore, as encouraging messages from organizations about the value of *all* employees' experiences and opinions, not just bosses'.

CHANGE THE SYSTEM!

The *talking* cure, the *training* cure, and traditional approaches to the *grading* cure all focus on transforming the brutal behavior of individual bosses, just as the *change the victims* approach seeks to inoculate individual workers against the ravages of abuse from above. To *change the system,* on the other hand, is to reform work arrangements for all bosses and all subordinates according to a new social compact, one that gives employees a greater voice in designing the operating environments in which they work.

Traditional work arrangements characteristically muffle workers' voices through the use of top-down decision-making, one-way channels of communication from bosses down to subordinates, and narrowly defined jobs that handcuff subordinates by instituting as much surveillance and as little autonomy as possible. *New York Times* journalist Louis Uchitelle wrote, accurately, that modern society's need to move to more effective, progressive work practices requires a "switch from the decades-old practice of dividing work into simple, repetitive tasks carried out by workers who are never greatly respected by their bosses, or trusted to perform without being prodded or policed."[9] The landscape of modern organizational life is dotted with alluring buds of progressive work arrangements, all structured to give employees greater influence in shaping the worlds in which they work.

INCREASING VOICE

"Flattened hierarchies," "seamless organizations," and self-managed teams[10] are examples of the new arrangements aiming to extend *voice* to workers. Efforts to create "action learning" in organizations[11] and to introduce "gainsharing,"[12] employee ownership,[13] circular structure,[14] total quality management (TQM), continuous improvement,[15] and process re-engineering[16] provide opportunities for workers' empowerment that lower barriers between bosses and subordinates. These fancy-sounding management tools, which seem mere structural reorganizations for the sake of efficiency, may in fact emerge as powerful means for shaping social perception and interpersonal behavior within organizations. Extending workers' voice through the implementation of progressive work arrangements and denying voice through the maintenance of more traditional work patterns and structures each make important statements about the social and human worth of employees.

Greater equalization of voice and representation among those on different rungs of the organizational ladder will lead to work environments where there are no longer *haves* and *have nots,* where *superior* and *inferior* are not presumed to fully define people, and where the position of "boss" becomes a matter of stewardship,[17] not an affirmation of pedigree. Abuse is discouraged when power is less one-sided; bosses' Darwinistic sense

of possessing and deserving elite status is met with less
institutional reinforcement; and subordinates' passivity
is reduced as their autonomy and self-esteem are increased.[18]

*Years ago, when I was just starting out in the firm, I
worked with a senior partner who, as they say, would
"brook no disagreement." He made decisions about our
work lives that affected our whole lives: how late we
would work; how early we would work; weekend work,
lunches, the whole bit. You would just receive notice.
What seemed worse was the way that he and other senior
partners would jerk us around, organizing and reorga-
nizing, moving people, dropping people, reassigning
projects without a word of explanation, much less fore-
warning. I've seen it happen now any number of times
with client firms. To me that's real abuse: treating people
like things which have no rights, no life, no need for self-
respect. There's them—up here—and all the rest of us
down there. "Hello, this is God telling you what to do"—
it's the firm's culture. When you're low on the totem pole
you're not a sentient, human being.*

*Now I'm one of them, a boss, and I find myself doing
the same thing. I looked in the mirror the other day, I
swear, and said out loud, "What a damned fool you are,
you're doing what others did to you." To tell you the
truth, it's embarrassing. But you get into positions, as
your career progresses, and you forget. You twist things
all around, justifying what you're doing. The crazy, awful
part is that I can offer you all sorts of reasons for why
they—down there—shouldn't be consulted or even informed.*

Letting go of traditional arrangements is not easy. But it can happen. When New United Motors assumed control of General Motors' Fremont Plant,[19] the administration sought to remove most distinguishing job classifications, closed a separate management dining room, and eliminated layers of management. Similar events reportedly occurred at Southwest Airlines, a current corporate success story. Observing that the company's pilots sometimes join the efforts of those who clean the airplanes, Professor of Management Charles O'Reilly concluded, "It signals a unity of purpose to the cleaning crew—that their work is as important as flying the plane."[20] It also discourages abuse of subordinates by collapsing status distinctions and creating a sense of teamwork.

The value of re-engineering, TQM, 360-degree feedback, and all the other examples of progressive work arrangements can be calculated only by taking into account *how* the arrangements are introduced as well as how fully the organization supports the nontraditional efforts.[21] Attempts to change organizations that are authoritarian, hierarchically oriented, or ingenuous negate the arrangements' worth as means of discouraging subordinate abuse, precisely because this sort of Machiavellian control is itself an abuse. Nowadays, for instance, brutal bosses may use progressive work arrangements as a cruel decoy for their harming of subordinates.

The point was illustrated during a conversation I had with a human resources professional at an organization that manages investments. Months before, the company had launched an effort to achieve cost-cutting and gains in efficiency through "process re-engineering," which, although it was expressly denied, seemed aimed at cutting personnel. Even before the elimination of as many as 30 percent of workers, the effects were corrosive. Work effort faltered throughout the organization as worried employees devoted increasing time to speculation about redundancy, and activity in the human resources group was no exception. Finally they were given the orders they had dreaded all along.

What's happening is cruel, deceptive, and dehumanizing. We were told to find redundancies. Target numbers were given to us, and if the redundancies didn't exist, we were told to create them: "Rewrite the job descriptions so that incumbents don't fit." And the re-engineering isn't even complete. The cuts are occurring in lower ranks, while new jobs are being created in upper ones. It's our responsibility to implement this fraud. People are suffering. I'm sick, physically sick, because of it. I'm so angry and hurt. I'm tired, and when I looked around me at the meeting, everyone around me was tired. We're standing in the middle of what feels like an enormous whirlpool.

Sanford has developed rashes; he has more than four dozen redundancies in his units. Mara is actually aging before my eyes. So many are frightened. It's not hard to see what's coming next. Reductions in operations personnel will justify reductions in us staff professionals once we carry out the execution. The new rules require that people being cut have no access to us. They cannot have any contact with people who knew them and whom they trusted in the past. Standing up and saying, "This is wrong and we shouldn't lie by rigging job descriptions, or abandon people by sending them away from familiar support personnel," is short-circuited by my boss. She must see what's happening, but still she says, "It's all

okay. We must support the effort." She's worried for her-
self. It's not safe to buck the system. These people are
acting as if all the rest of us are dunces, and are dispos-
able. They screwed up, then they decided how to fix it.
Their judgment is royal and the rest of us are here to
serve.

EMPTY TALK

Plenty of bosses talk empowerment, mass participation, and worker autonomy while behaving autocratically. Nowadays, it is organizationally correct to espouse
the virtues of progressive work arrangements. Companies
around the world are clamoring for workers to have
greater voice. Bosses in these companies give rehearsed
speeches on how team-style Japanese management con-
tributes to the success of "Japan, Inc." They identify
themselves as "coordinators" and "facilitators" and their
subordinates as "partners" and "associates." Statements
of organizational vision and purpose sound democratic
and appear everywhere on posters and laminated desk
plaques. But at day's end, beneficial consequences for
bosses' behavior and subordinates' experiences are much
harder to find.

In a 1994 study by Rath & Strong, 80 percent of the
managers surveyed claimed that employees should have
a greater role in facilitating change, but 40 percent of
them said they did not think that *their* employees were
capable of that kind of contribution.[22] Even more dismal
is the news turned up by a survey of one thousand *For-*
tune companies conducted by the University of Southern
California's Center for Effective Organizations: 68 per-

cent of the companies reported using self-managed teams, but their use affected a mere 10 percent of the companies' workers.[23] That discouraging finding is consistent with data from other investigations. Information collected by the Association for Quality and Participation, for instance, showed that although 70 percent of the one thousand U.S. companies surveyed said that they had employee involvement programs, fewer than 15 percent of the employees in those companies felt the programs' impact. And a January 1993 *New York Times* article[24] estimates that about 90 million employees, more than 70 percent of the labor force, still work under traditional work conditions.

Comfort might be found in the conception that all these data are only a snapshot of a trend's beginning, and that the percentage of workers affected by progressive work arrangements is gradually ascending. Aside from organizationally correct lip service, unfortunately, there is little evidence to support such a claim, and good reason to reject it. Efforts to extend and expand workers' voice and to cut down on abuse at the workplace are countered by three forces that act on bosses: *pressures* created by cycles of economic turbulence; *conflicting demands* concerning the exercise of power; and the *malignant motives* of individual boss personalities.

Cycles of economic change are an eternal dynamic of the marketplace. They put enormous *pressure* on business, government, and educational organizations, encouraging retreat from progressive work arrangements back to the "prodding and policing" of traditional ones. In a time of crisis due to declining financial prospects, Procter & Gamble moved away from using a team approach for sales-force development toward one that was more top-down.[25] And a return to old-fashioned work relations may even have occurred at Digital Equipment Corporation (DEC), a testimony to the influence of economic difficulties on bosses and corporations.

To students of business and companies, mention of DEC is likely to call to mind images of matrix management and consensual decision-making. DEC and such progressive work arrangements are like ham and eggs: The company's broad-minded approaches to work structure and labor relations were introduced by its founder, Ken Olson. For many years DEC's progressivism was identified as a leading contributor to its successes, and executives around the world pored over *Enfield: A High-Performance System,*[26] a 1984 publication that described the creation and management of a DEC production facility.

However, between 1990 and 1994 the company's fortunes declined and DEC reportedly lost around $4 billion. Ken Olson retired. On July 25, 1994, Robert B. Palmer, DEC's CEO, announced, "Matrix management at our company is dead."[27]Presumably, consensual decision-making was buried at the same funeral, and the company fell back on traditional work setups and patterns.

Criticizing organizations for turning back away from innovative work arrangements when times get tough can obscure an important point: *Organizations* are not doing the turning; individual bosses are. These bosses are simply choosing what is familiar over what is unfamiliar, preferring control to ambiguity—a natural and common reaction to crisis. Market crunches and organizational panics will always be part of the working world, as will this very human response to them, which will continue to block efforts to extend voice to all workers.

Defenders of traditional work arrangements will point accusing fingers at these pages and demand, "Do you want battlefield commanders to seek their troops' consensus in the midst of war? When a theater is on fire, shouldn't someone take over and lead the way out?" I would say *yes* to both questions, but *no* to the analogies that they attempt to draw. A crisis is not a crisis is not a crisis. Do not confuse the dimensions of *important* and *urgent* in judging the appropriate response to organizational emergencies. Not all crises, while important, have the urgency of a battle or a fire, and not all remedies require blunt, unilateral action. In fact, subordinates' input—as well as their risk-taking capacities, initiative, and commitment, which research clearly shows will all be diminished when they are deprived of voice and dignity—are usually required for a thorough and effective response to an emergency.

Paradoxically, for some bosses, the crush of economic difficulties has been aggravated rather than eased by the egalitarian credo of progressive work arrangements. They are faced with conflicting demands, at once held accountable for doing more with fewer resources and expected to do so without exercising the unilateral authority that once came with their positions. They are surrounded by demands to share power with those they once regarded as inferiors, while being pressed from above with mandates to meet intractable deadlines and an ever-more-severe "bottom line." Consequently, many bosses revert to endorsing in public progressive ideals that they ignore in private, and to putting so-called equals on frequent notice about who ultimately is *The Boss.*

Bosses' music, rather than their words, lets subordinates know how they are to dance. Gestures, tones, expressions, and other nonverbal cues send messages that are loud, clear, and intimidating—but not obvious violations of espoused commitments to fairness and against brutality. Without ever actually objecting to granting a voice to all workers, bosses can sandbag group decision-making and sully employees' reputations until defying their wishes is futile and dangerous. For many subordinates, abuse does not stop as organizations attempt to become more enlightened; it merely goes underground.

If an ideal transformation of a company is achieved, bosses are effectively retrained, systems are gradually changed, and bosses' abuse of subordinates may be constrained. But even these ambitious accomplishments cannot fully eradicate the negative potential of many bosses' cruel personalities and *malignant motives.*

For nearly a half century, from the time that the first studies on authoritarian personality and sadism[28] were conducted, evidence (including that which my colleagues and I have collected on abuse by bosses) has demonstrated that many people feel better when they make others feel worse. They are bullies, eager to exploit a power advantage by bludgeoning, belittling, and betraying those less powerful. Their emotional gain is not calibrated to the abuse's effectiveness in correcting any real or imagined problems; this is abuse for the sake of abuse. Malignantly motivated bosses experience relief and pleasure because they have harmed another human being. However organizations may be changed by the introduction of progressive work arrangements, the behavior of these bosses will remain the same. Giving all employees a voice in decisions and in the shaping of their work environments can discourage abuse on the job. But any announcement of the death of authoritarian hierarchies in organizations, or of an end to brutality, is more than premature: it's invalid.

Economic pressures and conflicting messages about control during turbulent times will always cause significant numbers of bosses, at every level, to embrace rather than shun the unprogressive methods that once were taken for granted. Even if it were otherwise, the promise of innovative and fair work arrangements would still be limited by the enduring presence of malignant flaws in human character. Organizational change and enlightenment should be avidly pursued, but their limitations, and the limitless toll of abuse on subordinates' well-being and productivity, require that something more be done.

Abuse of workers must be outlawed.

CONCLUSION:

Outlawing Brutal Bosses

I *was barely fourteen years old when I entered the green-*
grocer's shop. I'd carefully chosen my outfit for the occa-
sion: clean Levi Strauss jeans, shined combat boots, a
new red-and-white flannel shirt. After waiting until the
proprietor finished serving customers, I said quietly,
"You have a sign hung outside about a delivery boy's job.
If it's still open, I'd like it."

"You work for me, you got to know the rules." The man
had now turned around to face me.

Great, *I thought.* The money was badly needed. No
rules could be that bad: arrive on time; don't dawdle
while making deliveries; give the right change; be polite.

The shopkeeper leaned forward, put a finger into my
face, and announced loudly, "You're dreck"—*a Yiddish*

word for feces. The owner's wife, the butcher, and the butcher's assistant all looked away, either embarrassed by what was happening or smiling at my expense. Addressing the shop's three-person audience, the greengrocer restated his claim: "He's dreck. *Now I know it, you know it, and he knows it." He smiled self-approvingly. "That's the rule—you remember that you're* dreck. *You know what that means?* Dreck *is worthless. It's waste. When it smells too much, I flush it. When you smell, because you don't work how I want you to, you go too. Right down the toilet. Now,* dreck, *when I tell you, you do. When I don't tell you, you don't do! So,* dreck, *you want to work?"*

"Yes," I answered, thinking hard about what it would mean not to have income.

Arriving home, I passed a hallway mirror and saw my new red-and-white-checked flannel shirt and couldn't hold back any longer. Fighting the emerging tears, I locked myself in the bathroom and hid away, concealing my shame from anyone who might come home.

Every day my boss called me "dreck" and worse. Occasionally, when upset, he supplemented the name-calling with a tossed fruit or vegetable at my back. Going to work was torture. It occupied my thoughts as I sat in school, and it kept me awake at night. Stomach pains that developed after about three or four weeks on the job were diagnosed by a physician as a "spastic colon, from stress." I told my parents that it was school causing it, fearing that they'd make me quit the delivery job.

Later, when another job opened up and I was able to leave the greengrocer, I mentioned to some neighborhood people what had happened. My experiences were confirmed by witnesses as well as by others who had been similarly abused by this man. The community acted. The man was put on notice that the behavior would not be tolerated. He was going to be watched, and if he didn't stop, there would be consequences. And he improved. The greengrocer remained a lousy boss, but being surly was a step up from abusive.

Every human encounter contains potential for affirming or negating others' sense of worth and dignity. I learned this painfully as a boy at the greengrocer's shop. Tacit rules of behavior exist to regulate interpersonal relations and help define civility and fairness. Although the precise rules vary across the spectrum of world communities, their function is the same everywhere: They protect people in social encounters from damaging insults and personal harm. When community members obey the rules, it is likely that they will leave each encounter with positive feelings about themselves, others, and the experience itself. However, rudeness, injustice, and personal abuse cause the recipients to feel wounded and antagonistic toward both the encounter and the others involved.[1]

Forty years ago, the philosopher and theologian Martin Buber reflected on the affirmation or negation provided by human encounters. He concluded that the potential for each outcome invested human beings with a great responsibility in their dealings with one another. "The basis of man's life with man," he wrote, "is twofold, and it is one—the wish of every man to be confirmed as what he is, even as what he can become, by men; and the innate capacity in man to confirm his fellow men in this way. That this capacity lies so immeasurably fallow constitutes the real weakness and questionableness of the human race: Actual humanity exists only where this capacity unfolds."[2]

Almost twenty years later, the noted author and psychoanalyst Eric Fromm commented on the frequency and extent of people's failure to exercise this capacity. He wrote: "Mental sadism may be disguised in many seemingly harmless ways: a question, a smile, a confusing remark. Who does not know an 'artist' in this kind of sadism, the one who finds just the right word or the right gesture to embarrass or humiliate another in this innocent way."[3]

Fairness and basic respect in encounters with one another, however they may be defined by different communities, represent an unqualified minimum necessity of human conduct that applies to every member of a community. People's entitlement to just treatment is neither diminished by anyone's immediate needs or desires nor earned solely by work accomplishments or special personal attributes.[4] Violations of these elemental social guidelines implicitly denounce the victims as "outsiders." Thus, guarding against interpersonal abuse is a fundamental means of nourishing a community's cohesion.

Passing through an employer's gates complicates but does not alter the importance of mutual respect and justice in human affairs. In structured paper-and-pencil tests, open-ended questionnaires, face-to-face interviews, and spontaneous conversations, many hundreds of working men and women testified that accepting a job does not require relinquishing their right to be treated fairly and with civility. No matter the circumstance, bosses may not abuse others. They may not lie, restrict, or dictate employees' behavior outside the workplace, threaten harm, or protect themselves at the expense of those more vulnerable. Positions of greater power in organizations' hierarchy do not grant license to show favoritism, humiliate, or behave as masters or gods.

Stern, demanding bosses who insist on excellent performance may cause tension on the job, but this is not abuse, and working men and women recognize the difference. The difference, indeed, is distinct: Merely demanding bosses do not diminish feelings of self-worth and dignity, and do not produce such adverse personal effects as anxiety, depression, or lowered self-esteem. Employees strive to be given income, promotions, and perks in exchange for work achievements and productivity; but they expect to be treated fairly and with basic respect regardless of any contingencies. To believe—as some bosses do—that common decency is a reward, and not a right, is itself abuse.

Abuse on the job is a current affair. Turbulence in the economic environment of the 1990s has ignited explosions of brutality both from innate bullies who thrive on their mistreatment of others and from overburdened bosses who might never have behaved that way in less stressful times. The protection, dignity, and humanity of the workers at their mercy has too long been neglected. It is not the responsibility of the victims to alter their behavior, and it is very unlikely that the abusers will be inspired to alter theirs. The system itself must be the target of change.

Reforming the system that creates and sustains abuse is a feasible, vital, and—of course—daunting task. Workers' empowerment, basic dignity, and well-being must be reinstated, but this will take time and effort. Meanwhile, employees are suffering every day, all day long. They need, and deserve, defensive weapons against the double-siege of general nineties work pressures and the bosses who react to them with downright abuse.

SIX SURVIVAL SKILLS

The war of our workplaces will be over when on-the-job abuse is outlawed. In the meantime, years of interviews and analysis have revealed six survival skills that will keep bosses from brutalizing workers and workers from becoming prey.

1. *Know the Eight Daily Sins and when they're being committed.*
   Do not accept Deceit, Constraint, Coercion, Selfishness, Inequity, Cruelty, Disregard, and Deification as natural ingredients of relationships at the workplace.

2. *Recognize bosses for who and what they are.*
   Know your Dehumanizers, Blamers, Rationalizers, and their motives. Identify Conquerors, Performers, Manipulators, and the roots of their abuse. Note when and why they band together to protect one another at the expense of subordinates.

3. *Be aware of* Gotcha *goals.*
   Be alert to schemes and setups wherein discipline, rather than development, is the objective of employee supervision and monitoring. Adhere to the guidelines of effective electronic monitoring.

4. *Look around and reach out.*

The *change the victims* approach is fundamentally wrong, and will not remedy the misbehavior of abusers; however, it is instructive in its emphasis on workers' self-reliance and on the importance of peer support. Employees who are oppressed from above can move sideways to establish healthy and empowering bonds with fellow sufferers. Isolation is debilitating and is one of the causes and effects of abuse that can be overcome by reaching out.

5. *Focus on the accountability of bosses who abuse.*

The talking, training, and grading cures that the *change the abusers* approach advocates are unlikely to transform bosses and their habits, but they are worthwhile endeavors, and serve to make an important point: Bosses are uniquely responsible for the brutality that's poisoned our work environments.

6. *Watch yourself.*

Workers of all levels who act abusively toward subordinates are not justified or excused by their own mistreatment at the hands of *their* bosses. Apply the same categories and criticisms to yourself that you have administered to your boss. Look for yourself in the Brutal Boss Questionnaire. Uphold fairness, even in the face of unfairness. We all have the potential to be brutal bosses.

These six survival skills have as much to do with perception as they do with technique or active strategy, but that does not make them easier. Unlike other skills that prove helpful on the job, these are abilities that people possess outside of work and that are impaired, not improved, with more time spent in brutal work environments. Employees must regain the innate capacities for self-knowledge, self-protection, and self-assertion that are destroyed by the common and repeated cruelty of bosses.

Zealous advocates of managerial sovereignty at any cost may object to the idea of putting a stop to brutal bosses. They may argue that a boss's only guidelines for his or her treatment of subordinates should be business demands, personal opinion, and the owners' and stockholders' interests. They are wrong.

In an age when the processing of information is becoming *the* essential organizational asset, people's work behavior is central to competitive advantage as never before. Employees' initiative, unity, willingness to take risks, and commitment to the organization weigh in heavily along with technology and capital as determinants of company success. Organizations that permit abuse by bosses drastically decrease the value and effectiveness of their workers and their work. Human relations are not irrelevant to good business; they are part of its foundation.

I will not claim that organizations always fail when they cling to traditional work arrangements or harbor subordinate-abusing bosses. In reality, companies and businesses often survive, and even prosper, despite widespread mistreatment and regular humiliation of workers. In his book *The Reckoning,* a dramatic recounting of Henry Ford's treatment of his labor force, David Halberstam shows that Ford's behavior caused the suffering of many employees as the company's profits and market share continued to grow.[5] There were probably two reasons for this irony: one, innovations in product design and assembly gave Ford Motors undeniable technological advantages; and two, employees stayed on, despite the abuse, because of organizational loyalty and financial dependency.

Ford Motors made it big *despite* the injustice and abuse that went on in the workplace, not because of it. Organizational success does not require treading a path that harms employees. Injuries to lower-ranking individuals and to the spirit of institutions are pressing reasons to limit managerial sovereignty. Communities should have a compelling interest in protecting employees from brutality on the job, just as they have interest in boosting the profits that organizations bring into their midst; both serve the health, prosperity, and growth of the community at large.

When jobs are plentiful and employees mobile, protection of workers is not as urgent. Market forces will guide subordinates away from abusive organizations toward ones offering healthier work environments. These same forces will crush businesses whose internal, interpersonal abuses hinder their productivity, quality, cohesion, and Ford-like edge over competitors. But jobs in the late twentieth century are not plentiful, and workers are often trapped where they are by financial and employment fears. When their bosses turn on them with abuse, they are left without protection or recourse. Some avenue for redress outside of the organization must be available to subordinates suffering the harmful effects of abuse. Communities must oppose the mistreatment of workers and support their rights for equal human status. Protections are already offered to certain citizens who belong to specific ethnic, gender, and minority groups. It is time to extend this umbrella to working people everywhere.

Organizations that support and protect bosses by failing to take steps that discourage or punish their abusive acts should themselves face sanctions by their host communities. Employers have a duty to monitor, limit, and rectify the misconduct of people they have invested with power over others, diligently and deliberately. Outbursts and occasional cursing are not the cause of grievous harm to subordinates, nor are work pressures applied by stern and demanding bosses; yet when personal harm is incurred from bosses who cross the threshold of universal standards for fairness and decency, community sanctions are necessary.

Creating community sanctions to discourage brutality in organizations may seem odious. Ideally, people— bosses included—should voluntarily refrain from injuring one another. But, tragically, they do not. In that case, workers should be able to pursue corrective measures within their organizations, free from backlash and confident of a fair hearing and appropriate response. Yet they are not. Despite organizationally correct rhetoric about worker empowerment and mass participation, statistical evidence testifies that progressive work arrangements have improved the daily lives of very few employees. The system must be changed, reasonably and feasibly, by broadening our concept of the workplace to include and involve the community that houses it. In order to protect their citizens' welfare, communities must insist that organizations bear liability for bosses who conduct and condone harmful assaults on people who work for them.

Whether bosses treat their subordinates with basic respect or as prey alters both employees' well-being and the growth of successful enterprise. The fundamental requirements of human relationships are not suspended at organizations' front doors, nor are they adaptable to organizational crises, employee rank, or the designs and desires of those in powerful posts. Brutal bosses harm communities both at work and beyond by robbing citizens and institutions of their dignity and productivity. These costs cannot be tolerated.

Bosses who brutalize subordinates must be outlawed. Bosses everywhere, from *Fortune* fifty to greengrocers, must be put on notice. Communities are watching. There will be consequences.

APPENDIX:

The Brutal Boss Questionnaire

THE BRUTAL BOSS QUESTIONNAIRE

For an assessment of your current experience of abuse by superior(s) and its possible consequences for your health, well-being, and work productivity, complete the questionnaire that follows. Then find your personal rating using the scoring information which is provided on the reverse side.

Rate your boss on the following behaviors and actions. If you agree that a statement categorizes your boss, write a number from 5 to 8, depending on the extent of your agreement. If you disagree with a statement in reference to your boss, write a number from 1 to 4, depending on the extent of your disagreement.

1	2	3	4	5	6	7	8
strongly disagree						strongly agree	

1. My boss deliberately provides me with false or misleading information. ____

2. My boss treats me unfairly at times for no apparent reason. ____

3. My boss deceives me sometimes. ____

4. My boss deliberately withholds information from me that I need to perform my job. ____

5. My boss criticizes low-quality work from me. ____

6. My boss tells me how I should be spending my time when not at work. ____

7. My boss will "get" me if I don't comply with her/his wishes. ____

8. My boss humiliates me in public. ____

9. My boss calls me unflattering names. ____

10. My boss requires that her/his standards be met before giving a compliment. ____

11. My boss believes that I am generally inferior, and blames me whenever something goes wrong. ____

12. My boss acts as if s/he can do as s/he pleases to me, because s/he is the boss. ____

13. My boss treats me like a servant. ____

14. My boss expects me to dress appropriately at all times. _____

15. My boss treats me unjustly. _____

16. My boss steals my good ideas or work products and takes credit for them. _____

17. My boss will make me "pay" if I don't carry out her/his demands. _____

18. My boss displays anger publicly toward me by shouting, cursing, and/or slamming objects. _____

19. My boss criticizes me on a personal level rather than criticizing my work. _____

20. My boss demands that I give my best effort all the time. _____

21. My boss is tougher on some subordinates because s/he dislikes them regardless of their work. _____

22. My boss is discourteous toward me. _____

23. My boss is dishonest with me. _____

24. My boss shows no regard for my opinions. _____

25. My boss is deliberately rude to me. _____

26. My boss lies to me. _____

27. My boss misleads me for her/his own benefit. _____

28. My boss insists that I work hard. _____

29. My boss displaces blame for her/his own failures onto me. _____

30. My boss openly degrades and/or personally attacks me. _____

31. My boss mistreats me because of my lifestyle. _____

32. My boss demands that I constantly do high-quality work. _____

33. My boss reprimands me in front of others. _____

34. My boss deliberately makes me feel inferior. _____

35. My boss is not honest with the people who rank beneath her/him. _____

36. My boss threatens me in order to get what s/he wants. _____

(Scoring information on reverse side)

SCORING

Total your responses to the following questions:

#5: _____

#10: _____

#14: _____

#20: _____

#28: _____

#32: _____

TOUGH BOSS TOTAL: _____

Now total your responses to the remaining thirty questions.

BAD BOSS TOTAL: _____

KEY

Tough boss total +	*Bad boss total* =	*Assessment of boss*
Between 36 and 48	Less than 90	Tough, but not abusive
Less than 36	Less than 90	Not particularly tough
Between 36 and 48	Between 90 and 195	Tough, with instances of abuse. Adverse effects on work and well-being may very well occur.
Any	Greater than 195	Abusive. Deteriorating mental and physical health and lowered productivity are associated with this level of mistreatment.

NOTES

CHAPTER 1

1. A. Bryant. Jan. 16, 1993. "Behind the mutiny at Sunbeam-Oster." *New York Times,* L35 and L37.
2. A. Stanley. Jan. 9, 1993. "Zuckerman meets the troops." *New York Times,* L1 and L26.

CHAPTER 2

1. A. B. Fisher. Nov. 18, 1991. "Morale crisis." *Fortune,* 69–80.
2. B. Dumaine. Feb. 22, 1993. "The new non-manager managers." *Fortune,* 80–83.
3. Fisher, "Morale crisis."
4. S. Ratan. Oct. 4, 1993. "Why busters hate boomers." *Fortune,* 56–70.
5. S. Sherman. Jan. 25, 1993. "A brave new Darwinian work place." *Fortune,* 50–56.

6. A. Stern. July 18, 1993. "Managing by team is not always as easy as it looks." *New York Times,* section 3, p. 5.

7. J. A. Lopez. Oct. 6, 1993. "Firms force job seekers to jump through hoops." *Wall Street Journal,* B1 and B7.

8. L. Uchitelle. Jan. 31, 1993. "Stanching the loss of good jobs." *New York Times,* F1 and F6.

9. R. B. Reich. Dec. 19, 1993. "Companies are cutting their hearts out." *New York Times Magazine,* 54–55.

10. J. A. Byrne. May 9, 1994. "The pain of downsizing." *Business Week,* 60–69.

11. Reich, "Companies are cutting their hearts out."

12. Ibid.

13. J. Berger. Dec. 22, 1993. "The pain of layoffs for ex-senior I.B.M. workers." *New York Times,* B1 and B5.

14. P. T. Kilborn. Nov. 22, 1993. "Strikers at American Airlines say the objective is respect." *New York Times,* A1 and A8.

15. Ibid.

16. C. Duff. Jan. 11, 1993. "Jack the Ripper." *Wall Street Journal,* 1 and 14.

17. Reich, "Companies are cutting their hearts out."

18. *The Concise Oxford Dictionary.* 1964. London: Oxford University Press.

19. D. McShane. July 19, 1993. "Lessons for bosses and the bossed." *New York Times,* A15.

CHAPTER 3

1. B. Dumaine. Oct. 18, 1993. "America's toughest bosses." *Fortune,* 38–50.

2. D. Goleman. Dec. 28, 1986. "When the boss is unbearable." *New York Times,* section 3, pp. 1 and 29.

3. Ibid.

4. Dumaine, "America's Toughest Bosses." *Fortune,* 41.

5. Ibid, 39.

6. J. Bennett. Jan. 4, 1994. "Painful change at G.M. parts plant." *New York Times,* D1 and D7.

7. G. Rifkin. Jan. 23, 1994. "The 'Iron Lady' keeping Lotus on track." *New York Times,* F10.

8. J. Sexton. May 29, 1995. "Garment shop with a grand vision." *New York Times,* 23 and 24.

CHAPTER 4

1. S. G. Haynes and M. Feinlieb. 1980. "Women, work, and coronary heart disease: Prospective findings from the Framingham Heart Study." *American Journal of Public Health* 70, 133–41; A. Pine and E. Aronson. 1988. *Career Burnout: Causes and Cures.* New York: The Free Press; R. L. Repetti. 1987. "Individual and common components of the social environment at work and psychological well-being." *Journal of Personality and Social Psychology* 52, 710–20.
2. *Wall Street Journal* (April 4, 1995), 1.
3. T. A. Beehr. 1976. "Perceived situational moderators of the relationship between subjective role ambiguity and role strain." *Journal of Applied Psychology* 61, 35–40; J. S. House and J. A. Wells. 1978. "Occupational stress, social support, and health." In A. McLean, G. Black, and M. Colligan (eds.). *Reducing Occupational Stress: Proceedings of a Conference* (publication number 78–140), pp. 8–29. Washington, DC: U.S. Government Printing Office; R. A. Karasek, K. P. Triantis, and S. S. Chaudhry. 1982. "Coworker and supervisor support as moderators of associations between task characteristics and mental strain." *Journal of Occupational Behavior* 3, 181–200; Repetti, "Individual and common components of the social environment at work."
4. Repetti, "Individual and common components of the social environment at work."
5. The detailed empirical description of this work is available in H. A. Hornstein, J. Michela, A. Van Eron, L. Cohen, W. L. Heckelman, M. Sachse-Skidd, and J. L. Spencer. 1995. "Disrespectful supervisory behavior: Effects on some aspects of subordinates' mental health." Manuscript. Teachers College, Columbia University.
6. J. Michela, D. H. Flint, and A. M. Lynch. 1992. "Disrespectful supervisory behavior as a social-

environmental stressor at work." Paper presented at APA/ NIOST Work Stress Conference.

7. J. Brockner. 1988. *Self-esteem at Work,* Lexington, MA: Lexington Books; C. L. Staples, M. L. Schwalbe, and V. Gecas. 1984. "Social class, occupational conditions and efficacy-based self-esteem." *Sociological Perspectives* 27, 1, 85–109; P. Tharenou. 1979. "Employee self-esteem: A review of the literature." *Journal of Vocational Behavior* 15, 316–46.

8. Brockner, *Self-esteem at Work;* M. L. Schwalbe. 1985. "Autonomy in work and self-esteem." *The Sociological Quarterly* 26, 4, 519–35; Staples et al., "Social class"; Tharenou, "Employee self-esteem." J. R. P. French Jr., C. J. Tupper, and E. Mueller. 1965. *Workload of University Professors* (Cooperative Research Project no. 2171, U.S. Office of Education). Ann Arbor: University of Michigan. J. R. P. French Jr. and R. D. Caplan. 1972. "Organization stress and strain." In A. J. Marrow (ed.). *The Failure of Success.* New York: AMACOM.

9. E. Larson. Oct. 13, 1994. "A false crisis: How workplace violence became a hot issue." *Wall Street Journal,* 1 and 10.

10. P. T. Kilborn. May 17, 1993. "Inside post offices, the mail is only part of the pressure." *New York Times,* A1 and A15.

11. Ibid.

CHAPTER 5

1. S. Kiesler, J. Siegel, and T. W. McGuire. 1984. "Social psychological aspects of computer-mediated communication." *American Psychologist* 39, 1123–134.

2. J. R. Aiello. 1993. "Computer-based work monitoring: Electronic surveillance and its effects." *Journal of Applied Social Psychology* 23, 499–507.

3. J. R. Aiello and C. M. Svec. 1993. "Computer monitoring of work performance: Extending the social facilitation framework to electronic presence." *Journal of Applied Social Psychology* 23, 537–48; G. Bylinsky. Nov. 4, 1991.

"How companies spy on employees." *Fortune,* 131–40;
T. L. Griffith. 1993. "Monitoring and performance: A
comparison of computer and supervisor monitoring."
Journal of Applied Social Psychology 23, 549–72; J. Laabs.
1992. "Surveillance: Tool or trap?" *Personnel Journal,* 96–
104; D. M. Nebeker and C. B. Tatum. 1993. "The effects of
computer monitoring, standards, and rewards on work
performance, job satisfaction, and stress." *Journal of
Applied Social Psychology* 23, 508–36.
4. D. McGregor. 1960. *The Human Side of Enterprise.* New
York: McGraw-Hill.
5. H. Levinson. 1973. *The Great Jackass Fallacy.* Cambridge:
Havard University Press.
6. Laabs, "Surveillance: Tool or trap?"
7. Bylinsky, "How companies spy on employees."
8. Ibid.
9. S. Strom. Sept. 15, 1993. "K-Mart sued by 43 workers in
a privacy case in Illinois." *New York Times,* Business
Section, 3.
10. Aiello and Svec, "Computer monitoring of work
performance."
11. Bylinsky, "How companies spy on employees."
12. Laabs, "Surveillance: Tool or trap?"
13. Bylinsky, "How companies spy on employees."
14. Ibid.
15. Ibid.

CHAPTER 6

1. B. Dumaine. Oct. 18, 1993. "America's toughest bosses."
Fortune, 38–50.
2. J. B. Harvey. 1989. "Some thoughts about organizational
backstabbing: Or, how come every time I get stabbed in the
back my fingerprints are on the knife?" *Executive* III, 4,
271–77.
3. P. T. Kilborn. Nov. 22, 1993. "Strikers at American
Airlines say the objective is respect." *New York Times,* A1
and A8.

4. W. Boeker. 1992. "Power and managerial dismissal: Scapegoating at the top." *Administrative Science Quarterly* 37, 400–21.

CHAPTER 7

1. D. Goleman. Dec. 28, 1986. "When the boss is unbearable." *New York Times,* Business Section, 1 and 29; J. T. Knippen, T. B. Green, and K. Sutton. Dec. 1992. "Overcoming an intimidating boss." *Supervision,* 6–8, 13.
2. A. Pines and E. Aronson. 1988. *Career Burnout: Causes and Cures.* New York: The Free Press.
3. In H. Levinson (1978). "The abrasive personality." *Harvard Business Review,* 86–94, the following is advised: "Describe events to the boss, do not accuse or interpret his/her behavior; Ask the boss to reflect on his/her behavior's consequences by thinking about similar episodes in his/her own past; Encourage the boss to think about why he/she is attacking when there has been no attack."
4. D. Goleman. Sept. 16, 1990. "A constructive criticism primer." *New York Times,* Business Section, 23.
5. B. F. Skinner. 1971. *Beyond Freedom and Dignity.* New York: Knopf.
6. S. Sleek. 1994. "Corporate expert details how to fix the work place." *The Monitor: American Psychological Association,* 35.
7. E. E. Lawler III. 1990. *Strategic Pay.* San Francisco: Jossey-Bass; A. M. Mohrman Jr., S. M. Resnick-West, and E. E. Lawler III. 1989. *Designing Performance Appraisal Systems: Aligning Appraisals and Organizational Realities.* San Francisco: Jossey-Bass.
8. B. O'Reilly. Oct. 17, 1994. "360 degree feedback can change your life." *Fortune,* 93–100.
9. L. Uchitelle. Jan. 31, 1993. "Stanching the loss of good jobs." *New York Times,* Business Section, 6.
10. R. Beckhard and W. Pritchard. 1992. *Changing the Essence: The Art of Creating and Leading Fundamental Change in Organizations.* San Francisco: Jossey-Bass; W. G.

Dyer. 1977. *Team Building: Issues and Alternatives.*
Reading, MA: Addison-Wesley; J. R. Galbraith. 1994.
Competing with Flexible Lateral Organizations. Reading,
MA: Addison-Wesley; J. R. Galbraith, E. E. Lawler III, and
Associates. 1993. *Organizing for the Future: The New Logic
for Managing Complex Organizations.* San Francisco:
Jossey-Bass; J. Richard Hackman (ed.). 1990. *Groups that
Work (and Those that Don't): Creating Conditions for
Effective Teamwork.* San Francisco: Jossey-Bass; D. A.
Nadler, M. S. Gerstein, R. B. Shaw, and Associates. 1992.
*Organizational Architecture: Designing for Changing
Organizations.* San Francisco: Jossey-Bass.

11. C. Argyris and D. A. Schon. 1974. *Organizational
Learning: A Theory of Action Perspective.* San Francisco:
Jossey-Bass; P. Senge. 1990. *The Fifth Discipline: The Art
and Practice of the Learning Organization.* New York:
Doubleday Currency; K. E. Watkins and V. J. Marsick. 1993.
*Sculpting the Learning Organization: Lessons in the Art
and Science of Systemic Change.* San Francisco: Jossey-
Bass.

12. Lawler, *Strategic Pay.*

13. Y. Onaran. 1992. "Workers as owners: An empirical
comparison of intra-firm inequalities at employee owned
and conventional companies." *Human Relations* 45, 1213–
235.

14. R. L. Ackoff. 1994. *The Democratic Corporation:
A Radical Prescription for Recreating Corporate America
and Re-discovering Success.* New York: Oxford University
Press.

15. D. Ciampa. 1992. *Total Quality: A User's Guide for
Implementation.* Reading, MA: Addison-Wesley; P. R.
Scholtes. 1988. *The Team Handbook.* Madison, WI: Joiner
Associates.

16. M. Hammer. 1990. "Re-engineering work: Don't
automate, obliterate." *Harvard Business Review* (July–
August), 104–12.

17. P. Block. 1993. *Stewardship: Choosing Service Over Self-
Interest.* San Francisco: Berrett-Koehler.

18. J. Brockner. 1988. *Self-esteem at Work.* Lexington, MA:
Lexington Books; M. L. Kohn and C. Schooler. 1982. "Job

conditions and personality: A longitudinal assessment of their reciprocal effects." *American Journal of Sociology* 87, 1257–286; P. Thernou. 1979. "Employee self-esteem: A review of the literature." *Journal of Vocational Behavior* 15, 316–46.

19. J. Pfeffer. 1992. *Managing with Power.* Boston: Harvard Business School Press.

20. B. O'Reilly. June 13, 1994. "The new deal." *Fortune,* 50.

21. M. Hammer and S. A. Stanton. 1995. *The Re-engineering Revolution.* New York: Harper Business; H. Lancaster. Jan. 17, 1995. " 'Re-engineering' authors consider re-engineering." *Wall Street Journal,* B1.

22. B. P. Noble. March 6, 1994. "On bosses, barriers and beliefs." *New York Times,* Business Section, 25.

23. B. Dumaine. Sept. 5, 1994. "The trouble with teams." *Fortune,* 86–92.

24. Uchitelle, "Stanching the loss of good jobs."

25. P. A. Galagan. Aug. 1992. "Beyond hierarchy: The search for high performance." *Training and Development,* 21–25.

26. Barbara Perry was the author of this volume, which was produced by DEC.

27. G. Rifkin. July 25, 1994. "Digital shows doctrine the door." *New York Times,* Business Section, 1 and 6.

28. T. W. Adorno, E. Frenkel-Brunswick, D. F. Levinson, and R. N. Sanford. 1950. *The Authoritarian Personality.* New York: Harper & Bros.; E. Fromm. 1973. *The Anatomy of Human Destructiveness.* New York: Holt, Rinehart & Winston.

CONCLUSION

1. E. Goffman. 1955. "On face work: An analysis of ritual elements in social interaction." *Psychiatry,* 213–31; E. Goffman. 1967. *Interaction Ritual: Essays on Face-to-Face Behavior.* New York: Pantheon Books; E. Goffman. 1971. *Relations in Public.* New York: Basic Books.

2. M. Buber. 1957. The William Alanson White Memorial Lectures, Fourth Series. *Psychiatry* 20, 95–130.

3. E. Fromm. 1973. *The Anatomy of Human Destructiveness.* New York: Holt, Rinehart & Winston.

4. In contrast, during the 1993 mayoral race in New York City, an opponent of one candidate defended his uncivil behavior by saying: "It feels good to dish out abuse. Besides, the enemy has sacrificed his right to be treated like a fellow human being—to be treated civilly, that is." (In W. Grimes. Oct. 17, 1993. "Have a #%!&$! day." *New York Times,* B7.)

5. D. Halberstam. 1986. *The Reckoning.* New York: Morrow.

BIBLIOGRAPHY

Ackoff, R. L. 1994. *The Democratic Corporation: A Radical Prescription for Creating Corporate America and Rediscovering Success.* New York: Oxford University Press.

Adorno, T. W., Frankel-Brunswick, E., Levinson, D. F., and Sanford, R. N. 1950. *The Authoritarian Personality.* New York: Harper & Bros.

Aiello, J. R. 1993. "Computer-based work monitoring: Electronic surveillance and its effects." *Journal of Applied Social Psychology* 23: 499–507.

Aiello, J. R., and Svec, C. M. 1993. "Computer monitoring of work performance." *Journal of Applied Social Psychology* 23: 537–48.

Argyris, C., and Shon, D. A. 1978. *Organizational Learning: A Theory of Action Perspective.* San Francisco: Jossey-Bass.

Beckhard, R., and Pritchard, W. 1992. *Changing the Essence: The Art of Creating and Leading Fundamental Change in Organizations.* San Francisco: Jossey-Bass.

Beehr, T. A. 1976. "Perceived structural moderators of the relationship between subjective role ambiguity and role strain." *Journal of Applied Psychology* 61: 1, 35–40.

Bennett, J. Jan. 4, 1994. "Painful change at G.M. parts plants." *New York Times,* D1 and D7.

Berger, J. Dec. 22, 1993. "The pain of layoffs for ex-senior IBM workers." *New York Times,* B1 and B5.

Bies, R. J. 1987. "Beyond voice: The influence of decision maker justification and sincerity on procedural fairness judgments." *Representative Research in Social Psychology* 17: 3–14.

———. 1987. "The predicament of injustice: The management of moral outrage." *Research in Organizational Behavior* 9: 289–319.

Bies, R. J., and Schapiro, D. C. 1988. "Voice and justification: Their influence on procedural justice." *Academy of Management Review* 31: 676–85.

Block, P. 1993. *Stewardship: Choosing Service Over Self Interest.* San Francisco: Berrett-Koehler.

Boeker, W. 1992. "Power and managerial dismissal: Scapegoating at the top." *Administrative Science Quarterly* 37: 400–421.

Brockner, J. 1988. *Self-esteem at Work.* Lexington, MA: Lexington Books.

———. Winter 1992. "Managing the effects of layoffs on survivors." *California Management Review:* 9–28.

Bryant, A. Jan. 16, 1993. "Behind the mutiny at Sunbeam-Oster." *New York Times,* L35.

Buber, M. 1957. The William Alanson White Memorial Lectures, Fourth Series. *Psychiatry* 20: 95–130.

Bylinsky G. Nov. 4, 1991. "How companies spy on employees." *Fortune:* 131–43.

Byrne, J. A. May 9, 1994. "The pain of downsizing." *Business Week:* 60–69.

Carey, P. M. Winter 1993. "Do the right thing." *Your Company:* 6–7.

Ciampa, D. 1992. *Total Quality.* Reading, MA: Addison-Wesley.

Collins, G. Aug. 15, 1994. "Tough leader wields the ax at Scott." *New York Times,* D1 and D2.

Cooper, C. L., Dyck, B., and Frolich, N. 1992. "Improving the effectiveness of gainsharing: The role of fairness and participation." *Administrative Science Quarterly* 37: 471–90.

Cordes, C. L., and Dougherty, T. W. 1993. "A review and integration of research on job burnout." *Academy of Management Review* 18: 621–56.

Cowan, A. L. Jan. 17, 1994. "Unmourned departure at Coopers." *New York Times,* D1 and D8.

Duff, C. Jan. 11, 1993. "Jack the Ripper." *Wall Street Journal,* 1 and 4.

Dumaine, B. Feb. 22, 1993. "The new non-manager managers." *Fortune:* 80–83.

———. July 25, 1994. "A knockout year." *Fortune:* 94–102.

———. Oct. 18, 1993. "America's toughest bosses." *Fortune:* 38–50.

———. Sept. 5, 1994. "The trouble with teams." *Fortune:* 86–92.

Dyer, W. 1977. *Team Building: Issues and Alternatives.* Reading, MA: Addison-Wesley.

Finchman, F. D., and Jaspers, J. M. 1980. "Attribution of responsibility: From man the scientist to man the lawyer." In L. Berkowitz (ed.). *Advances in Experimental Social Psychology: Vol. 13*, pp. 81–138. New York: Academic Press.

Fisher, A. B. Aug. 23, 1993. "Sexual harassment: What to do." *Fortune:* 84–88.

———. Nov. 18, 1991. "Morale crisis." *Fortune:* 70–80.

Fitzgerald, L. 1993. "Sexual harassment: Violence against women in the workplace." *American Psychologist:* 1070–76.

Fromm, E. 1973. *The Anatomy of Human Destructiveness.* New York: Holt, Rinehart & Winston.

Galagan, P. Aug. 1992. "Beyond hierarchy: The search for high performance." *Training and Development:* 21–25.

Galbraith, J. R. 1994. *Competing with Flexible Lateral Organizations.* Reading, MA: Addison-Wesley.

Galbraith, J. R., Lawler, E. E. III, and Associates. 1993. *Organizing for the Future: The New Logic of Managing Complex Organizations.* San Francisco: Jossey-Bass.

Goffman, E. 1955. "On face work: An analysis of ritual elements in social interactions." *Psychiatry* 18: 213–31.

———. 1967. *Interaction Ritual: Essays on Face-to-Face Behavior.* New York: Pantheon Books.

———. 1971. *Relations in Public.* New York: Basic Books.

Goleman, D. Dec. 28, 1986. "When the boss is unbearable." *New York Times,* 1 and 29.

———. Sept. 16, 1990. "A constructive criticism primer." *New York Times,* F23.

Greenberg, J. 1990. "Looking vs. being fair: Managing impressions of organization justice." In B. M. Staw and

L. L. Cummings (eds.) *Research in Organizational Behavior: Vol. 12* (111–57). Greenwich, CT: JAI Press.

———. 1990. "Organization justice: Yesterday, today, and tomorrow." *Journal of Management* 16: 399–432.

Greenberg, J., and Folger, R. 1983. "Procedural justice, participation, and the fairness process effect in groups and organizations." In P. B. Paulus (ed.) *Basic Group Processes* (235–56). New York: Springer.

Greenhouse, L. March 2, 1993. "Justices to decide if psychological injury is needed to prove sex harassment." *New York Times,* A17.

———. Nov. 10, 1993. "Court, 9–0, makes sex harassment easier to prove." *New York Times,* A1 and A22.

———. Oct. 14, 1993. "Ginsberg at fore in court's give and take." *New York Times,* A1 and B8.

Griffith, T. L. 1993. "Monitoring and performance: A comparison of computer and supervisor monitoring." *Journal of Applied Social Psychology* 23: 549–72.

Grimes, W. Oct. 17, 1993. "Have a #%!&$! day." *New York Times,* section 9, 1 and 7.

Gross, A. Aug. 1993. "The boss who made me pack his underwear." *Ladies' Home Journal:* 98–102.

Hackman, R. J. (ed.). 1990. *Groups that Work (and Those that Don't): Creating Conditions for Effective Teamwork.* San Francisco: Jossey-Bass.

Hamilton, D. L. 1980. "Intuitive psychologist or intuitive lawyer? Alternative models of the attribution process." *Journal of Personality and Social Psychology* 39: 762–72.

Hammer, M., and Stanton, S. A. 1995. *The Re-engineering Revolution.* New York: Harper Business.

Harvey, J. B. 1988. *The Abilene Paradox and Other Meditations on Management.* Lexington, MA: Lexington Books.

———. 1989. "Some thoughts about organizational backstabbing: Or, how come every time I get stabbed in the back my fingerprints are on the knife?" *Executive* III: 271–77.

Henkoff, R. Jan. 10, 1994. "Getting beyond downsizing." *Fortune:* 58–64.

Hoffman, J. Nov. 10, 1993. "Plaintiffs' lawyers applaud decision." *New York Times,* 22.

Hornstein, H. A., Michela, J. L., Van Eron, A. M., Cohen, L. W., Heckelman, W. L., Sachse-Skidd, M., and Spencer, J. L. 1995. "Disrespectful supervisory behavior: Effects on some aspects of subordinates' mental health."

Unpublished manuscript, Teachers College, Columbia University.

Keisler, S., Siegel, J., and McGuire, T. W. 1984. "Social psychological aspects of computer-mediated communication." *American Psychologist* 39: 1123–134.

Kilborn, P. T. March 15, 1993. "New jobs lack the old security in a time of disposable workers." *New York Times,* A1 and A15.

———. May 28, 1994. "In a growing number of stores hidden security microphones are listening." *New York Times,* A6.

———. Nov. 22, 1993. "Strikers at American Airlines say the objective is respect." *New York Times,* A1 and A8.

Knippen, J. T., Green, T. B., and Sutton, K. Dec. 1992. "Overcoming an intimidating boss." *Supervision:* 6–8, 13.

Kohn, M. L., and Schooler, C. 1982. "Job conditions and personality: A longitudinal assessment of their reciprocal effects." *American Journal of Sociology* 87: 1257–286.

Laabs, J. 1992. "Surveillance: Tool or trap?" *Personnel Journal:* 96–104.

Lancaster, H. Jan. 17, 1995. " 'Re-engineering' authors consider re-engineering." *Wall Street Journal,* B1.

Larson, E. Oct. 13, 1994. "A false crisis: How workplace violence became a hot issue." *Wall Street Journal,* 1 and 10.

Leventhal, H., and Tomarken, A. 1987. "Stress and illness: Perspectives from health psychology." In S. V. Kasl and C. L. Cooper (eds.) *Stress and Health: Issues in Research Methodology.* New York: Wiley.

Levinson, H. 1973. *The Great Jackass Fallacy.* Cambridge: Harvard University Press.

———. 1978. "The abrasive personality." *Harvard Business Review:* 86–94.

Lind, E. A., Kurtz, S., Mussante, L., Walker, L., and Thibaut, J. 1980. "Procedural and outcome effects on reactions to adjudicated resolution of conflicts of interest." *Journal of Personality and Social Psychology* 39: 643–53.

Longenecker, C. O., and Scazzero, J. A. Jan. 1993. "Creating a climate for quality." *Supervision:* 14–16.

Lopez, J. A. Oct. 6, 1993. "Firms force job seekers to jump through hoops." *Wall Street Journal,* B1 and B7.

McGregor, D. 1960. *The Human Side of Enterprise.* New York: McGraw-Hill.

McShane, D. July 19, 1993. "Lessons for bosses and the bossed." *New York Times,* A15.

Michela, J., Flint, D. H., and Lynch, A. M. Nov. 1992.

"Disrespectful supervisory behavior as social-environmental stressor at work." Paper presented at American Psychological Association NIOST Work Stress Conference.

Mohrman, A. M. Jr., Resnick-West, S. M., and Lawler, E. E. III. 1989. *Designing Performance Appraisal Systems: Aligning Appraisals and Organizational Realities.* San Francisco: Jossey-Bass.

Moskowitz, M. May 14, 1993. "Spare the knife, spoil the company." *New York Times,* A31.

Nadler, D. A., Gerstein, M. S., Shaw, R. B., and Associates. 1992. *Organizational Architecture: Designs for Changing Organizations.* San Francisco: Jossey-Bass.

Nebeker, D. M., and Tatum, B. C. 1993. "The effects of computer monitoring, standards, and rewards on work performance, job satisfaction, and stress." *Journal of Applied Social Psychology* 23: 508–36.

Noble, B. P. Aug. 15, 1993. "New reminders on harassment." *New York Times,* F25.

———. July 10, 1994. "Questioning productivity beliefs." *New York Times,* F20.

———. March 6, 1994. "On bosses, barriers and beliefs." *New York Times,* F25.

———. Sept. 19, 1993. "Dissecting the 90's workplace." *New York Times,* F21.

O'Reilly, B. June 13, 1994. "The new deal." *Fortune:* 44–52.

———. Oct. 17, 1994. "360-degree feedback can change your life." *Fortune:* 93–100.

Onaran, Y. 1992. "Workers as owners: An empirical comparison of intra-firm inequalities at employee-owned and conventional companies." *Human Relations:* 1213–235.

Pfeffer, J. 1992. *Managing With Power.* Boston: Harvard Business School Press.

Pickering, J. W., and Matson, R. E. May 1992. "Why executive development programs (alone) don't work." *Training and Development:* 91–95.

Pines, A., and Aronson, E. 1988. *Career Burnout: Causes and Cures.* New York: The Free Press.

Psychology Today. (July/August 1989). "The 'absent boss' syndrome." 24–25.

Ratan, S. Oct. 4, 1993. "Why busters hate boomers." *Fortune:* 56–70.

Reich, R. B. Dec. 19, 1993. "Companies are cutting their hearts out." *New York Times Magazine,* 54–55.

Repetti, R. 1987. "Individual and common components of the social environment at work and psychological well-being." *Journal of Personality and Social Psychology* 52: 710–20.

Rifkin, G. Jan. 23, 1994. "The 'Iron Lady' keeps Lotus on track." *New York Times,* F10.

———. July 25, 1994. "Digital shows doctrine the door." *New York Times,* D1 and D6.

Rosenthal, A. M. Oct. 26, 1993. "On my mind: On civil respect." *New York Times,* A21.

Sashkin, M., and Williams, R. L. 1990. "Does fairness make a difference?" *Organization Dynamics* 19: 56–71.

Schellhardt, T. D. Oct. 6, 1993. "Managing your career." *Wall Street Journal,* B1.

Schminke, M. 1993. "Consequences of power in a simulated job: Understanding the turnover decision." *Journal of Applied Social Psychology* 23, 52–78.

Scholtes, P. R. 1988. *The Team Handbook.* Madison, WI: Joiner.

Schwalbe, M. L. 1985. "Autonomy in work and self-esteem." *The Sociological Quarterly* 26: 519–35.

Seltezer, J., and Numerof, R. E. 1988. "Supervisory leadership and subordinate burnout." *Academy of Management Journal* 31: 439–46.

Senge, P. 1990. *The Fifth Discipline: The Art and Practice of the Learning Organization.* New York: Doubleday Currency.

Sexton, J. May 29, 1995. "Garment shop with a grand vision." *New York Times,* L23 and 24.

Sherman, S. Jan. 25, 1993. "A brave new Darwinian workplace." *Fortune:* 50–56.

Sleek, S. 1994. "Corporate expert details how to fix the workplace." *Monitor: American Psychological Association* 35.

Smith, L. Aug. 9, 1993. "What the boss knows about you." *Fortune:* 88–93.

———. July 25, 1994. "Burned-out bosses." *Fortune:* 44–52.

Stanley, A. Jan. 9, 1993. "Zuckerman meets troops." *New York Times,* 1 and 26.

Staples, C. L., Schwalbe, M. L., and Gecas, V. 1984. "Social class, occupational conditions and efficacy-based self-esteem." *Sociological Perspectives* 27: 85–109.

Stern, A. L. July 18, 1993. "Managing by team is not always as easy as it looks." *New York Times,* C5.

Strom, S. Sept. 15, 1993. "Kmart sued by 43 workers in a privacy case in Illinois." *New York Times,* D3.

Swaboda, F. July 27, 1993. "Conference tries to define 'high-performance' jobs." *Washington Post,* D1 and D5.

Tharenou, P. 1979. "Employee self-esteem: A review of the literature." *Journal of Vocational Behavior* 15: 316–46.

Trevina, L. K., and Ball, G. A. 1992. "The social implications of punishing unethical behavior: Observers' cognitive and affective reactions." *Journal of Management* 18: 751–68.

U.S. Congress Office of Technology. 1987. "The electronic supervisor: New technology, new tensions." Washington, DC: U.S. Government Printing Office.

Uchitelle, L. Jan. 31, 1993. "Stanching the loss of good jobs." *New York Times,* F1 and F6.

———. Aug. 8, 1993. "Union leaders fight for a place in the President's workplace of the future." *New York Times,* A32.

———. July 27, 1993. " 'Empowering' labor held key to more jobs." *New York Times,* D1 and D9.

Watkins, K. E., and Marsick, V. J. 1993. *Sculpting the Learning Organization: Lessons in the Art and Science of Systemic Change.* San Francisco: Jossey-Bass.

Harvey Hornstein is a professor of social-organizational psychology at Columbia University Teachers College and has served as a consultant to senior management groups throughout the world for more than twenty years. A former director of the National Training Laboratories' Center for Professional Development and a practicing psychotherapist, he lives in New York City.